RETIREMENT
MONEY
MANAGEMENT

Case Studies of People Who Retired
Successfully Even With a Small Nest Egg
(and others who didn't and why)

CAROL JACKSON TAYLOR

Copyright © 2020, Carol Jackson Taylor

All rights reserved. No part of this publication may be reproduced, distributed or transmitted in any form, or by any means, including photocopying, recording, or other electronic or mechanical methods, without the prior written permission of the author, except in the case of brief quotations embodied in reviews and certain other non-commercial uses permitted by copyright law. All the names, characters, and incidents that appear in this book have been changed to protect the identities of any real persons. Any resemblance to actual people, places or events is coincidental.

Scripture quotations from the ESV® Bible (The Holy Bible, English Standard Version®), copyright © 2001 by Crossway Bibles, a publishing ministry of Good News Publishers. Used by permission. All rights reserved.

Scripture quotations from the New Revised Standard Version of the Bible, copyright © 1946, 1952, and 1971 National Council of the Churches of Christ in the United States of America. Used by permission. All rights reserved worldwide.

Scripture quotation from THE HOLY BIBLE, NEW INTERNATIONAL VERSION® NIV®Copyright © 1973, 1978, 1984 by International Bible Society®Used by permission. All rights reserved worldwide.

Book design by FormattedBooks.com

DEDICATION

The older I become, the more I realize how much my parents taught me by their sound example. They took me to church as a little girl and taught me to tithe 10%. They also taught me to save. Each week I put 10% of my little allowance into my piggy bank.

These two principles formed the basis of my adult life and eventually led to the success I enjoyed in my career. I feel so fortunate that my parents taught me as they did.

I, in turn, have taught my children and grandchildren the same lesson. A strong tradition passed down through the generations.

TABLE OF CONTENTS

. . . .

CHAPTER ONE
    ELDERLY AND ALONE – WITH NO NETWORK 1

CHAPTER TWO
    DON'T LET YOUR KIDS DRAIN YOUR ASSETS 18

CHAPTER THREE
    INVEST THAT DIVORCE SETTLEMENT FOR YOUR
    RETIREMENT 28

CHAPTER FOUR
    KNOWLEDGE IS GOLD 40

CHAPTER FIVE
    PLANNING IS KEY 49

CHAPTER SIX
    FAMILY DEALINGS: A STUDY IN RELATIONSHIPS 58

CHAPTER SEVEN
    SUCCESSFUL MANAGERS 69

. . . .

INTRODUCTION

How much money have you saved towards your retirement? Do *You* think it's enough?

The average amount saved in corporate retirement funds such as a 401(k) is around $103,000. Balances in IRAs and ROTH IRAs are approximately $107,000 according to reports from 2019. On average, 'experts' calculate retirees need between $1million and $1.6 million to retire comfortably. That's a pretty large short-fall.

The following pages show examples of real people who were my clients just a few years ago. Their names and identifying circumstances have been changed, but the case studies remain accurate. Some had more than $100,000 and others had the same or less, but they were able to live comfortably until their deaths if they simply planned properly. You will also see clients that did not plan and why their results were not successful.

With over 30 years' experience working in the financial markets, I encountered many different situations from market highs to market crashes. I also encountered people who had money in the markets with no concept of how markets work. They were totally at the mercy of their stockbroker who was in the business solely to make money.

Throughout this book, you will notice that I do not recommend specific stocks, bonds, or products because over time these change. Some products that I recommended to my clients in this book no longer exist or are no longer being used as I used them.

When I first met with a client, I used a yellow legal pad and pencil to take notes about their investment expectations and what their risk tolerance was. Then I used that pad and pencil to sketch what their proposed portfolio of investments would look like and how it should perform. Clients understood this because it was simple. Of course, I was required to give clients brochures, prospectuses, and other materials, and explain them; but clients didn't understand these and simply took them home and put them in a file drawer never to be viewed again.

This book points out the mistakes my clients made so they will be evident and not made by you. The stock, bond, or annuity is not as important as the reason behind it. Not everyone is a good money manager or a good planner, but I believe this book will show you how to avoid big blunders. This book will also show you what to look for in choosing an honest stockbroker and how to avoid the 'salesmanship' of financial charlatans.

MARKET CRASHES I WORKED THROUGH			
YEAR	%LOSS	LASTED	RECOVERY
1987	29.6%	3 months	Sept. – Nov. 1987
1998 Tech Bubble	15.4%	2 months	Sept. – Nov. 1998
2000 9/11 Attack	44.7%	25 months	Sept. 2000 - 2002
2008-2009 Housing Crisis	50.9%	16 months	Nov. 2007 – Feb.
2020 Covid19	29% ??	???	????

The above figures vary between reporting data, but the point is that markets will go down and then rebound. That has been the case since the infamous 'crash' of 1929.

CHAPTER ONE

ELDERLY AND ALONE – WITH NO NETWORK

Some clients were my favorites over others, because of the rapport built over the years. Mary Ellen was such a client. She and I had many things in common and I always enjoyed her company. Before her retirement, she had been a businesswoman for many years. She had a quick grasp of finances and kept informed about world events as well as economics. She would ask me intelligent questions and never tried to second-guess my recommendations.

I knew she was a careful money manager and would not fall for a scam. Additionally, over the years I knew her family wouldn't try to get her money before her death and knew her handyman wasn't taking advantage of her. These are all important facts to investigate when managing the money of a person that is aging, becoming frail, and needing more help.

When I seriously considered my retirement, I knew I couldn't leave clients like Mary Ellen and a few others defenseless. I feared some brokers would take advantage of such clients if given a chance and I felt an obligation to remain their advisor to the end. I'm not sorry.

> *"Therefore I tell you, do not worry about your life;*
> *for tomorrow will bring worries of its own.*
> *Today's trouble is enough for today."*
> Matthew 6:25-34 NRSV

I acquired Mary Ellen as a client when I was still working at a large brokerage firm. A younger broker was leaving and Mary Ellen was his new client. He told me he thought I would be a good fit for Mary Ellen since she was an 'older' woman and he wanted to be sure that I took good care of her. He had developed a good rapport with her, but had not made any changes to her account.

I made an appointment with Mary Ellen and she came to my office. I was pleasantly surprised to see a tall, slender, stylish woman with a firm handshake who didn't appear to be the typical 'older' woman. Her dark hair, streaked with silver, waved around her face and she was stylishly well dressed. A very pretty woman, I thought. She was 74 years of age.

Another broker in the city had managed her portfolio and it was losing money each month. She was right in being concerned at her age. Unfortunately, he had invested her in bond funds and then interest rates began rising and her portfolio lost a lot of value. He was advising her to hold tight until the rates went low again, but she was nervous and afraid she would lose more money.

After discussing her financial situation, I learned her husband died several years before; she survived cancer and retired from her long-term career. As for her tax situation, she had a long-term loss carry-over from a previous brokerage firm before the one she was with at the time of our visit. She was frightened at all the losses and wanted to know how she could stop the draining of her portfolio.

I suggested stopping further losses by selling her current bond mutual funds. Then I recommended she invest the money in government mortgage bonds that were paying quite well at that time and provided a good degree of safety. She agreed. The government bonds worked very well for her portfolio providing the income she needed. She was able to relax.

When I opened my independent business office, she followed me as a client and we continued a wonderful association over the years. She had no children of her own but maintained a strong relationship with her stepson and his family in another state. She and I ultimately attended the same church and it was always delightful to see her there on Sundays.

One of the things I always loved about her was her giggle. It was infectious–almost like a young schoolgirl. I treasured that sound and still hear it in my memory as I write about her.

She developed a hobby of working with stained glass and making wall hangings. She made one for me as a gift–a beautiful fish making bubbles in the deep blue sea. Towards the end of her life, she gave me another made of clear, beveled glass. Hanging in the sunlight it gives a myriad of rainbow hues. These are both priceless to me.

After a few years, I placed her money into a variable annuity, which gave her some exposure to stocks to keep up with inflation. The annuity offered guaranteed withdrawals that she could not outlive. It also allowed her to grow her investment in good market years and protected her against loss of principal in down market years. She was able to take a larger monthly income withdrawal from the annuity, which helped her feel more secure. She also had a small IRA that we placed in another variable annuity. She only took the Required Minimum Distribution from that annually.

Mary Ellen lived in a modest three-bedroom brick home where she spent countless hours in her gardens, and they were beautiful. She employed a handyman to keep the yard trimmed and help her with minor projects around the house.

She developed a wonderful friendship with another widow, Denise. Mary Ellen quickly introduced us so her friend could become my client as well. They were like two teenagers, laughing, traveling, and having a delightful time together. Their adventures lasted about 5 years; then Denise did not wake up one morning. She had a heart attack during the night. Mary Ellen was devastated. It wasn't long afterward before Mary Ellen's health began to fail–nothing too drastic, but she began having problems with balance and double-vision.

After Denise's death, Mary Ellen began looking for a secure place to live. I'm sure she was afraid to die alone. Once she called and asked my advice about a reverse mortgage that she saw advertised on television, thinking she might need more money. But I advised against it. She didn't need the money at that point and probably never would. She asked my opinion about living in an assisted living facility. I told her I didn't feel that was necessary unless she wanted the company of other people her age. She had always been alone and wasn't a very social person. My answers seemed to satisfy her for the moment.

About a year later she decided she would move closer to her brother further north in the state. She put her house on the market and rented an apartment near him, moving most of her furniture; but then her house would not sell. So, she moved back into her home since she didn't want to rent it and could not afford to keep both the house and apartment.

Two years later, she called to tell me she had arranged to move to an assisted living facility. We changed all the addresses on her accounts and she expected to be happy and safe. But, after two months, I received a call with her distinct giggle. She was back at home because she hated living at the assisted living facility. She told me she detested the food, didn't want to play Bingo and the women were cliquish. I reassured her that I would reverse all the addresses on her accounts and that I agreed with her decision. She would be fine in her home.

Several times, she called to ask if I was certain she would not outlive her money. I would calculate the money she had, divide it by the amount she withdrew each month and tell her she would definitely run out when she was 125 years old or so. She would giggle, say thanks and hang up, reassured!

Her health began to deteriorate further. She gave up driving and could no longer ride her exercise bike. She didn't work with her stained glass anymore. Even so, she was always upbeat–never whiney or complaining.

In time, she arranged for a caregiver through an agency to come to her home daily to help her with tasks. Unfortunately, that person and several others afterward stole groceries from Mary Ellen as well as her credit card. It wasn't worth the hassle to her, so she let them all go.

There were visiting nurses and a person from the Council on Aging that kept trying to get her to go to a nursing home, but she refused. They even talked to me one time when I was visiting her, hoping I would convince her to go into a nursing home. But I knew she was still capable of living within her home. Her handyman built a ramp to cover the two steps between her living room and kitchen area. He kept her lawn and outside areas in repair, took out her trash, shopped for her groceries; but most importantly, he checked on her daily. She was able to cook simple meals, feed her cat and make coffee. Furthermore, she was still in her right mind. We would talk on the phone often and several times, I visited her during these difficult times.

One day she called to tell me her daughter-in-law and grand-daughter were coming to see her and she was so excited. Incredibly, while they were there, Mary Ellen was admitted to the hospital and died in a few days. It was opportune timing since her only remaining family was there to make all arrangements for her burial and take care of the house.

She was efficient and independent to the end. When she died, Mary Ellen was 93 and still had over $100,000 left! She was more than a client–she was a good friend.

ACTION POINTS:

- Mary Ellen did almost everything correctly. Before she became my client, she had two other stockbrokers that lost a lot of money for her–both in 'safe' bond funds. Diversification of her investments into both bonds and stocks or even jumbo CD's could have saved her from such losses.

- Moving out of her house before selling it was a mistake–she should have remained in it until it sold. She didn't lose a lot of money during this time but she could have avoided the physical and mental anguish of two moves.

- Fortunately, she cut her losses early when she moved into and out of the assisted living facility. Had she remained much longer, she would have been miserable.

- She should have thoroughly researched both of those moves in advance, but hindsight is always 20/20.

Even to your old age and gray hairs
I am he, I am he who will sustain you.
I have made you and I will carry you;
I will sustain you and I will rescue you.
Isaiah 46:4 NIV

• •

An 'elderly orphan' would be a good term to describe those people we encounter who are displaced into an environment they aren't familiar with. They have no spouse, children, or close relatives and are hanging on by a thread. Illness, lack of income, and sometimes a language barrier often complicate their situation. They have no one to name as a durable or medical power of attorney, no one to advocate for them and no one to dispose of their remains. Yet, somehow, they manage to survive. Luci was such a person.

Luci and I first met in 1991 through a quirk of fate. One day the #800 line mixed up in our firm and delivered calls from all over the United States into our south Texas office. I had just hung up with a call from California when my phone rang again.

A lilting voice with a heavy accent began asking me questions about investments. I soon ascertained she was elderly with no concept of anything more complicated than bank C.D.'s. It was an exercise in patience trying to explain the difference between mutual funds and bonds to her. She was right to be confused about how her call to an office in central Texas had reached me in south Texas. "But, can I do business with you?" she asked. "Of course!" I answered. And so began a remarkable relationship.

She called me regularly. "Hello, Carol? This is Luci," each call began. Her accent made it difficult for her to communicate. I would patiently explain statements and reports to her repeatedly until she understood. "OK, thank you!" she would breezily say as she hung up.

Luci was very private–almost secretive–but as months passed; she divulged a few facts to me. She was on kidney dialysis three days a week. She didn't own a car. This meant she walked several blocks to the bus stop, waited in the sweltering heat, and rode to a seedy neighborhood clinic for her treatment. Her next day was recuperation and then it was time for another treatment. She sent me the name of her attorney and hospital she normally used in case something went wrong. She often had problems with her dialysis graft. The graft required hospitalization for surgical repair on several occasions.

She projected a celebrity air even though she owned a small condominium in a declining neighborhood. Her conversations were always thought-provoking. She despised Clinton, worried about the economy, and was a strong Christian. Many times, she would tell me she was praying for my husband and me. I assured her of my prayers for her too, especially when she was having trouble with her dialysis.

Luci, in due course, revealed she had performed in operas in both New York and Europe. She and her husband traveled the world, but she was now divorced with no children. She alluded to being part of a very glamorous lifestyle, but gave few details. When I would ask too many questions, she would brush them aside with, "Oh, I don't want to talk about it anymore."

She loved New York City and lived there in comfort until she decided in the 1980s to move to Texas with close friends. Once moved, her friends didn't like the heat so they sold their condominium and moved back to New York. Luci tried, but couldn't sell hers for even close to what she had paid for it. She could not afford to return to New York. She was stranded–an opera star in south Texas.

Luci had few friends in Texas. Nieces and nephews in Mexico didn't contact her once they discovered she was in poor health without much money. An animal lover, she contributed small bits of money to animal welfare groups, but had no pets of her own. Her greatest desire was to visit New York, but she knew she couldn't afford it.

Luci was my client for several years before it was necessary to meet. I pictured a small, gray-haired lady with a sweet smile. Arriving in her neighborhood early, I stopped by a coffee shop to pass the time. My eyes were drawn to a woman with bleached blond shoulder-length hair, sunglasses, and bright red lipstick who appeared to be in her seventies. She looked rather out of place in the coarse surroundings. Well, you guessed it. Later when I arrived at Luci's that same woman opened the door! Fortunately, I maintained my composure as I adjusted my expectations. After all–I was dealing with a New York Opera Star!

Her condominium was small, but elegantly decorated with a pristine white sofa, original art pieces, tasteful curios, and beautiful faux gold-trimmed mirrors. Luci was petite–almost bird-like–her hands fluttering as she talked. Her skin was smooth with very few wrinkles and she was still a pretty woman–although the blond hair was not flattering. We talked about her dialysis–how had she been able to survive over 20 years? She related at length how she visited the library to educate herself about the procedures. She closely monitored what she ate and kept a close eye on the technicians so the treatment process was precise. She told of others at the same clinic that had died–but she was determined to live.

We finished our business and I offered to take her to lunch. She agreed and chose Luby's Cafeteria as her favorite restaurant. Once there, she selected several dishes plus dessert and ate every bite–all the while talking about her doctors, the treatments, and her beloved New York City.

The new investments I arranged on that visit enabled her to increase her monthly income. She was amazed at her new fortune and began planning a summer visit to New York. She stayed in the apartment of a friend who had gone to Europe. Her dialysis was nearby and she almost crowed at being back in 'her city'. Another summer she traveled to San Francisco. Each time she would send me a lovely postcard. She also began taking a taxi to a clinic in a better neighborhood for treatments. Her health improved as well as her mental outlook.

She confided more as time went on. Her attorney was old and was hoping her estate would go to him so we took steps to ensure that he would not receive more than his normal fees. Another time she thought her doctor at the clinic was in love with her. She would laugh as she told me how he flirted with her or how she knew he looked forward to seeing her each time. This went on for quite a while until she later changed clinics. I wondered if the infatuation was true or only her imagination.

In the summer of 2001, she became convinced she was dying of cancer because of terrible pains in her stomach. She began giving away many of her possessions and preparing for death. She told me she had made cremation arrangements but did not know what would happen to the ashes. I asked if she would like me to scatter them. "Where?" she asked. "Oh, I could scatter them in the Gulf," I replied. "Oh, no!" she cried, "I'm afraid of the water!" "Well, how about in the Texas Hill Country or someplace pretty where the wildflowers bloom?" I asked. She thought that might be acceptable and we never discussed it further.

My husband and I visited her a few weeks later. Luci was thrilled to meet him and twittered around him girlishly. She asked if we could take her to the mall to buy face cream. We discovered she was too short to get into my SUV, so Bill literally picked her up and lifted her in. She was ecstatic! Off we went where she followed her walker through the high-end store looking at this and that before selecting an expensive cream. It must have worked well since her skin was still smooth and beautiful–especially at her advanced age.

Then she announced she wanted to eat at Luby's again so we did. She ate a sizable meal taking some home for later enjoying every morsel. She flirted shamelessly with Bill telling him how handsome he was, smiling brilliantly at him and touching his arm being coy and flattering at the same time. It was a fun day.

During the September 11 crisis, I phoned her to reassure her about her investments. "How are you feeling?" I asked. "Oh, I'm fine," she replied. "I don't have cancer, so I guess I'm going to live!" However, she didn't sound over-joyed about it. She had told me several times earlier that she was tired–she was ready to die.

Then in November, I received a call from a nephew in Mexico asking if I knew where she was–her message machine was full and he could not find her.

I began calling hospitals and finally located her. When I was able to talk to her, I discovered she had fallen and broken her hip. She was terribly angry with God for allowing it to happen. "I did everything right!" she stormed, "And now this! How could He do this to me?" I tried to soothe her but it did no good. I told her I would pray for her, "Thanks!" she spat.

A few days later when I phoned, she seemed less annoyed at God, but her old spirit was gone. Her sentences would trail off as though she were drugged and drifting off to sleep. She rallied a bit and then whispered "Bye, Bye."

Social workers began calling for financial information, a guardian was appointed, and soon she was placed in another facility for rehabilitation. But, it wasn't to be. She died December 1, 2001.

After a few weeks, I met the guardian at a small restaurant to pick up her ashes. He laughed that he had 'taken Luci to breakfast' that morning on his way to meet me. I, in turn, 'took her to lunch' and she 'occupied a corner of my office' for a few weeks until the wildflowers reached their prime. I felt she would have approved of and enjoyed all the activities.

The guardian also gave me two CD's of a recital Luci had given in 1963. She would have been 38 years of age. Her voice was beautiful–a soprano–rich and vibrant. I tried to imagine what she looked like those many years ago; dark eyes, long black hair, small and lovely. I played the CD's in my office while Luci's ashes were nearby–it seemed like a suitable eulogy.

Texas bluebonnets were in full bloom surrounded by Indian paintbrush, wine cups, and yellow daisies all bursting with brilliant color when we arrived in the Hill Country. A gusty wind blew and the sky was overcast. It was Good Friday. "That ashes may return to ashes and dust to dust and the imperishable spirit, refined as by fire, may be forever with the Lord…" I read from "A Service for Cremation". After a brief prayer, my husband opened the small bag of ashes and they rode the wind, wafting over the beautiful flowers. Tears suddenly filled my eyes at the memory of my little friend. I would surely miss her phone calls, our visits, along with her indomitable spirit and will to live.

ACTION POINTS:

- Luci should have never moved from New York City, where she was financially comfortable, had friends and medical connections. She was totally out of her comfort zone and became disconnected from her friends and lifestyle. She could not afford to return, so she merely existed in an environment she detested. Drastic moves like this should be avoided in later life especially if the person is ill and alone.

- She was fortunate no one took advantage of her financially.

    Her attorney was too old but kept her on as a client
    Her remaining nephews and nieces were in another country and not interested
    She had no friends to call in an emergency
    No one knew her situation because she was so secretive

- She should have found another attorney, a bank trust officer, or someone she could confide in that could be her power of attorney. She wanted me to help her in that regard, but by law, registered financial advisors cannot serve in that capacity.

· ·

Women often tend to be people-pleasers. They regularly put their own lives on hold to help others–be it family members or friends. They pretend to agree with others repeatedly to their detriment. Pleasers are easy targets for salespeople since they usually buy the product offered. They don't want to decline and cause bad feelings.

Pleasers agree to burdens of extra responsibilities at work, allow their friends to over-load them with requests for help, and in general neglect their own needs to provide for others. This is not an admirable quality but one that is rooted in the desire for affirmation because of low self-esteem. The client view below is a perfect example.

*The simple believe anything, but the prudent
give thought to their steps.*
Proverbs 14:15 NIV

Nancy telephoned me one day to make an appointment. Another client of mine gave her my name with a strong recommendation. That is always a superb way to acquire a new client!

She was an interesting woman–well-spoken, and had a doctorate in engineering. The corporation she worked for provided her with superb benefits and security. She was not married and had no children. She had been investing for many years, but was unhappy with the returns she was receiving. Therefore, we set an appointment to meet at my office.

At our first meeting, Nancy arrived carrying a stack of papers and statements. We went through the many investments she currently owned that had been 'sold' to her by various stockbrokers. Some she had owned for over 20 years and they had no value. Her stockbroker kept telling her to hang on to them because they would increase in value someday. That 'day' had never come.

After our first meeting, I did a proposal for her of what I would change and replace. I also proposed what her portfolio would look like and how I expected it to perform if she chose me to manage her money. I put everything in writing with charts and graphs explaining all aspects. She liked my suggestions so we began a long broker-client relationship.

She owned a collection of gold coins, limited partnerships, and other junk investments that took me years to unwind. She could only recover pennies on the dollar for what she had invested in the beginning. The limited partnerships sent tax statements annually with information she was required to include in her tax return. They were nothing more than a headache. She never recovered her investment in the gold coins but ended up storing them in her safety deposit box for the future.

She also had some older annuities, mutual funds, and a fair amount of money in her 401(k) with her employer. Additionally, she had other retirement plans from former employers, some of which she had already rolled over into IRAs. She had also funded a ROTH IRA over the years.

Nancy had done a superb job of saving money for her retirement. Though she was very intelligent, she had little knowledge of how to invest her money or how to *plan* for her retirement. She was forever calling me to ask about a particular stock she read about–a new pharmaceutical drug that was going to make millions, a new corporation that had no track record of accomplishment or a foreign oil company that was going to solve the entire world's energy problems. I would oblige just in case they had merit, but then explain to her why an untested drug or foreign oil company might not be the best investment she should make for her future.

She toyed with retiring in a few years. She asked my advice about moving to Arizona or New Mexico to help her bad allergies. I encouraged her to make plans to retire. Since she had plenty of money–she might as well enjoy it. Yet, she never made any move to retire. She would remain for one more year at the corporation even though she no longer enjoyed her position.

One of Nancy's best friends was June, who also became a client of mine. When June received a cancer diagnosis, Nancy agreed to become her caregiver until her death. June named Nancy to settle her estate, which involved all her possessions, investments, plus her house. Additionally, June was the 'guardian of the person' for another woman who had been in a nursing home for years. When June died of cancer, Nancy became the successor manager of this woman's care. She told me she could not retire and leave the state until this woman died because she had promised June to care for her. That only involved an occasional visit to make sure her treatment was suitable, trimming her nails and taking care of any financial paperwork that needed attention.

Later, when this woman eventually died, Nancy also inherited the rest of her estate. So money kept flowing in while Nancy continued working and her retirement dreams kept getting dimmer.

Meanwhile, I invested her money in two managed accounts–one for her personal money and the other for her retirement funds. I also did her taxes so I could manage her portfolio for tax purposes. Nancy needed extra tax help with June's house that she inherited because she decided to keep it as a rental property. It became a constant worry of acquiring responsible tenants plus upkeep and repairs.

Nancy's continual concern was cancer. Her mother and brother had both died of cancer and she was terrified of receiving that diagnosis. She had regular checkups and many false positives, but she was always clear after rechecks. She was working with a noted doctor who had monitored her for years but when Nancy reached age 70, the doctor told her to stop worrying. Since she had avoided cancer up to this point, it was doubtful she would ever have it.

Unfortunately, about one year later she received the diagnosis of breast cancer. She immediately had a double mastectomy and began treatment with massive doses of chemotherapy followed by radiation. When I saw her afterward, she was a shadow of herself. She did recover to a point but then began having symptoms of Parkinson's and mild dementia.

Of course, that meant she had to retire since she was no longer able to go into her office and handle the administrative duties of her position. Yet, there was no joy in retirement because she spent all her time going for treatments and doctor's appointments.

It was at this point she began the process of revising her will. Since her friend, June, and several others she knew had experienced a successful outcome of appointing a friend or friends to manage their end of life care, she decided she would do likewise.

When we began our client relationship, she had roughly $500,000 and when she began to plan her caretaker beneficiaries, she had over $2 million. She had only distant relatives left in her family, so they could be no help in her care. Consequently, she chose seven close friends to be her beneficiaries in exchange for their promise to care for her until her death.

We discussed the details of this at great length, choosing beneficiaries and allocating her estate in varying amounts of money depending upon each beneficiary's responsibility. She revised her will several times and switched beneficiaries around to suit her frame of mind, which changed often.

I retired before Nancy's death. Since this prearrangement worked for two of Nancy's friends that needed end-of-life care and had no family, I am hopeful it worked for Nancy. At least it gave her peace of mind that she had done all she could to plan her final days in the care of good friends and not strangers.

ACTION POINTS:

- Nancy had a doctorate, so she should have been capable of critical thinking. So why did she allow previous financial advisors to load her up with "flavor of the day" investments? She owned gold, limited partnerships dealing with apartment developments, oil wells, and other questionable financial products. She should have thoroughly researched these investments. She lost a lot of money on them all.

- Nancy should have developed a plan for retirement. She had plenty of money saved for a comfortable retirement, but she never took the time to design a plan. Where would she live in retirement, where did she want to travel, what new events did she want to experience when retired? She let the years pile up until her health was gone and she became trapped.

- She did not want to allow a bank trust department to manage her money or end of life care. Banks can be very impersonal but she could have appointed a trusted friend to consult on the personal comforts of her care naming them a 'guardian of the person'. Having individuals appointed to provide care in return for receiving an inheritance can be problematic. Those individuals might become overwhelmed with decision-making or become ill themselves and be unable to continue. If Nancy was not coherent enough to make changes in her care instructions at that point, those named people would still inherit at Nancy's demise but she would have no one left to watch over her end-of-life care.

CHAPTER TWO

DON'T LET YOUR KIDS DRAIN YOUR ASSETS

....

Widows seem to get the short end of the stick, especially if the husband was married before and has children. I do not blame a person in a second marriage for protecting their children. There are so many stories of the 'new' wife shutting out the children of the first marriage and converting all the husband's assets to her children or vice versa. With an ironclad will and a good attorney, this would be impossible. Still, it seems that few ever do the proper planning to avoid this mistake.

It is usually up to the woman to make sure what the outcome is in the event of the husband's premature death or even divorce. Prenuptial agreements help protect assets in the event of divorce and wills or living trusts help protect the surviving spouse. Have these talks before tying the knot.

> *"Train up a child in the way he should go; even when he is old he will not depart from it"*
> Proverbs 22:6 ESV

....

Mutual friends introduced Julia to me and she was a delightful person to know. She seemed delicate, fragile, with short red hair, and brilliant blue eyes. Her voice was melodic and I found out later she had been quite the vocalist in her early years. Her style of dress was classic and her clothes fit like a glove over her slender figure. She had the mannerisms of a refined woman and yet was down-to-earth and very friendly and easy to get to know.

She was a recent widow and still having difficulty getting through her grief. Her husband had been a doctor with a large practice. They had married later in life since he was a widower and she was divorced. He had two grown children and she had three grown children. Julia and her husband enjoyed a happy marriage and especially enjoyed traveling in the US and abroad. He collapsed and died at her feet as they were leaving the house for the airport to embark on another trip. She was shattered and barely able to function after what happened. Confused by all the details that followed in settling his estate, she worried about how she would survive in the aftermath.

When she found out I was a financial advisor, she wanted to visit further to see if I could help or give any advice about what she should do going forward. She invited me to her home to discuss ideas. She lived in a well-kept brick ranch of the 70's era splendidly furnished with art and other items from their world travels.

Julia asked if I would like a cup of tea. She proceeded to prepare the tea in a heated teapot with loose tealeaves in the English manner and served it with fresh-baked pastries. Even the cups and saucers were bone china–she was a gracious host!

She told me on our first visit that her husband's will left the house to her for her lifetime but if she sold it, she would receive 1/3 of the sale proceeds with the remainder going to his two children. She also inherited a small rental unit elsewhere in town that needed extensive remodeling and a reliable tenant. Her late husband's practice was not marketable but she needed to sell the building that housed it. Again, the proceeds were to split into thirds along with his children. She told me what her monthly Social Security survivor's benefit was and it was very generous.

Julia was completely lost about what to do with his IRA, which she inherited as well as another investment account. I knew the broker on the accounts she had, so I called him with her permission, and inquired about her portfolio position. I was surprised when he told me he was going to be leaving that firm very shortly and suggested I should have her become my client and transfer her accounts to my company. He thought we would be a good fit because she needed extensive help and had no idea what to do with her money. So, with his blessing, that's what we did, and an excellent relationship began.

On one visit, she told me about her family as she was growing up. They were all part of a Christian singing group, Julia, her 2 sisters, and parents. They sang Gospel music together for many years. She still loved music and she was very involved in her church choir.

Julia always listened to Christian radio and television. It is unfortunate, but one signature of Christian radio and television is the ads and commercials encouraging listeners to buy gold and silver. These metals are promoted to be lifesavers when the economy or today's currencies collapse. Julia would call me from time to time, telling me about listening to certain programs that were predicting the world's ruin and the need for gold or silver coins–what should she do? We would discuss it and I would tell her that buying gold was for investors who had account balances much larger than hers. For instance, how much gold would she need to buy a loaf of bread if the world's economy collapsed? She would realize that answer was plausible and not the program. So, she would hang up the phone until the next program or preacher piqued her mind.

She told me after a while that her three children hounded her for money. Two of her daughters had no money sense and her son had no ambition. Also, it was not long until her late husband's two children began pressuring her to sell the house so they could have the remainder of their inheritance. She wavered–wanting to remain where she was and yet wanting to keep the peace. We calculated her 1/3 portion that would be realized from the sale of her home and found it would not be sufficient to purchase another home or condominium. She appeased herself that she wasn't sure she wanted the responsibility of homeownership and all it entailed and that maybe she would be happier renting an apartment.

Her oldest daughter lived in the northern part of the state, and was in the middle of a contentious divorce. She had four children and was forever battling for child support and help caring for them, and calling Julia for financial help. Julia finally decided she would move into an apartment closer to her daughter so she could be available to help when needed.

Julia began unwinding the life that she had so carefully built–church, friends, and a beautiful home with many wonderful memories. The real estate market was not very robust. There was no resale value to her lovely artwork or travel souvenirs, but she persisted until she was able to sell and move. She gave many treasures away because she had no room to take them.

Her money was dwindling because of her generosity to her children. The daughter she moved to help promised she would always take care of her mother in repayment for the help Julia had given her. However, I wondered, since she was unable to support herself, how would she manage to help her mother?

The apartment she selected was pleasing and appeared to be in a safe area, but quite small. I visited her several times over the next few years. She was never very happy. She missed her friends and church. I began getting more phone calls from her. She had a couple of minor fender benders and worried that if she had major car problems or a bad accident, she would not have the money to buy another car. Then what would she do? She also worried about losing her license and her ability to drive if she kept having accidents.

Then her memory began getting spotty and she would call to see what investments she owned and what her balances were. A little later, when visiting her daughter's home, she fell and broke her hip. I was fearful of that consequence, but she recovered and did not miss a beat physically. Yet, about a year later, her daughter thought she should go into assisted living because of her memory problems. Julia agreed to go without a whimper. We talked by telephone several times after she moved into the home and she sounded happy. She told me about several people there she was helping with their meals and newspapers. I believe she enjoyed being around other people since she was so lonely and she did not want to be a burden to her daughter.

Her daughter remarried a nice man who made it his purpose to watch over Julia. He took an active interest in her care. He and I spoke several times and Julia gave him a Power of Attorney to discuss her money with me. She had very little money left by this point and her mind was almost gone. Julia and I talked a few times by telephone, but she wasn't sure who I was or why I was calling. Still, she was the sweet person she had always been with a melodic voice–always gracious and polite.

Her son-in-law had to cash in her account to pay for her care. I didn't question it, since the amount left was quite small. I knew they would need money for her assisted living care and eventual nursing home care if she lived that long. We lost touch after that, so I don't know how long she lived, but I doubt it was very long.

Julia was a delightful client as well as a friend. She was a devout Christian and trusted God for everything. I am certain He took care of her and she is now singing in a heavenly choir.

ACTION POINTS:

- Julia and her second husband should have created wills that protected each other from their children of previous marriages. Unfortunately, he left her with financial problems to manage such as the disposal of his office property and the run-down condominium in town. She was not very proficient at handling those difficulties and was under pressure from his children to sell before she was ready.

- If Julia had been stronger-willed and not agreed to her own children's constant requests for money or capitulated to his children's urging to sell and divide the proceeds of her lovely home, she could have remained in a secure situation with her friends and support network. But, she was a pleaser–and she ended up being the one who was not pleased.

- Julia did not have enough money to afford the purchase of long-term care insurance. In most cases of this type, once a patient is in a home and their money runs out, between their Social Security and Medicaid, they can remain. This does involve some pre-planning because not all homes accept Medicaid.

· ·

Many of my clients were cagey at first about their families. They would brag on their children and grandchildren and nothing was ever wrong in their sunny little world. But, in time, they would begin to confide their fears to me about what would happen to their kids once they were gone. Their kids did not have any desire to be thrifty, stay out of debt, or learn to live within their means.

Some would tell me that one child would be fine with the money inherited but that the other one would spend it immediately. Others worried about the person their child had married fearing they would soon divorce and their child would lose the inherited money. Others had a closer relationship with their daughter-in-law than they did with their son, because he never had time for them and did not seem to care at all. It was difficult for me to navigate their fears and still devise beneficiaries for my clients' accounts.

*"A foolish son is a grief to his father,
and bitterness to her who bore him."*
Proverbs 17:25 ESV

When I first met Janet, my first impression of her was that she was an unhappy woman. She wore a continual frown; she was crabby, cynical, and did not have a pleasant personality. We met because of a talk I had given at a social group and she later contacted me to make an appointment to discuss her investments. She told me she had a broker in another state, but was thinking she should have one closer to where she lived. I agreed.

She lived in a dreary apartment–dreary because she kept the draperies closed with only minimum lighting inside. She was in her late 60's, with short, permed hair, little makeup and drab, dated clothing, and shoes. She still drove in the area to buy groceries and visit doctors. She was forever hoping to find a few bridge partners. Playing bridge and watching a little TV was her existence. Her life was very simple and she did not desire more. I could tell, though, she was a survivor.

As we talked, I found she had moved to our state from Alabama and had previously lived in one of the eastern states where she and her husband acquired numerous shares of local utility companies. They had retired to Alabama and then he died shortly thereafter, leaving her with a portfolio she did not understand. Her Alabama broker did not have a license in our state, so she was completely confused about what to do next. Her husband had stressed to her how important the utility stocks were that they held for many years, and told her she should not ever sell them.

As I reviewed her assets, I realized some of the utility stocks she held weren't any longer producing the income she relied upon nor were their ratings that acceptable. One or two were actually on the verge of bankruptcy with their dividends severely cut. She suspected something was wrong with those stocks because her income was down. It took me several months to get her account moved to my company, the stocks sold and the money placed in an account so we could make decisions on how best to move forward.

Janet also needed someone to advise her on taxes since she had always had them done in Alabama. I began doing her taxes, which allowed me to plan her investments accordingly and minimize her taxes.

From time to time, she would mention her children–she had two daughters and a son. Both daughters were a big disappointment to her. One daughter had never held a good job and had little ambition. The other daughter had married a man who soon became disabled, lost his job, and had no income. She was responsible for supporting them both and was not doing a very good job of it. Both of these children were constantly begging their mother for money–although they were both in their late 40's.

Her son held a job most of the time and his wife also worked, but he was a spendthrift, had a high debt load and they both lived beyond their means. He had a brief period of unemployment that worried her, but he was soon able to secure a new position in the northern part of our state and moved there. Janet was so disappointed in them all. The children were not raised this way since she and her husband never lived irresponsibly. She could not understand how they had become so undependable. Whenever they would ask her for money, she would first tell them she could not afford it and then they would beg and beg with a sad tale, until eventually she would give in. She knew the routine, expected it, and yet was mad at herself for giving in each time. The kids all knew her "hot buttons" and used her unmercifully.

I was able to devise a conservative portfolio for her that would provide additional monthly income. All was well for the time being. A few years later, she decided to move to the northern part of the state to be closer to her son and entered an assisted living facility. At that time, we decided it would be best to move the money into an annuity, which would preserve her principal and give her a higher monthly income to cover the added expense of assisted living. Her annuity would also give her the benefit of naming beneficiaries rather than passing through a will.

As she and I went over the various beneficiary payout options, she heard me explain there was a 20-year payout option. "Do you mean that my beneficiaries wouldn't get their money immediately but over 20 years?" she asked. "Yes", I answered. She was so relieved. "Let's do that!" she said without hesitation. She knew that once her children received their inheritance money, it would be spent instantly and they would have nothing left. She was worried about what would happen to them after she was gone, and this extended beneficiary period provided her with the assurance they would have money for a longer period.

Thankfully, we had the annuity in place before the market collapse that occurred after 9/11. The stock market closed for an entire week after the attack that destroyed the New York Twin Towers. Once the markets re-opened for trading, most stocks dropped and did not recover for quite some time. That was a very difficult period for the markets and investors. However, Janet's annuity kept her income secure.

Janet died in 2006, her principal intact, and her beneficiaries provided for over 20 years. The children were not happy to learn what she had done, but it assured them a regular monthly income for 20 years rather than giving them a large sum of money to spend irresponsibly.

I felt satisfied with a job well done. Janet's mind was at ease by providing her a stable income while she lived and a constant income for her children over the next 20 years.

ACTION POINTS:

- Janet's children constantly badgered her for money. She managed to keep her assistance to them at a minimum, but it was a perpetual problem.

- Rather than her children watching over her, Janet had to watch over them or at least worry about their future well-being.

- Janet's husband did her a disservice by not explaining their investments and then cautioning her never to sell the stocks. He may have thought they were a good investment, and they probably were at the time, but many investments lose their luster if not managed properly. It is difficult to sell or dispose of something that a deceased spouse tells you to keep.

CHAPTER THREE

INVEST THAT DIVORCE SETTLEMENT FOR YOUR RETIREMENT

....

Divorcees can be strange creatures. They fight long and hard to save their marriages and contend through attorneys for the best possible settlement. Then, quite a few of them do everything within their power (subconsciously or consciously) to get rid of the money. Why? I am sure there are as many reasons for this behavior as there are grounds for divorce. Still, as a financial advisor, I found it amazing.

The divorce settlement may be the last chunk of money they will ever have to help them find a new career or prepare for their retirement. Women simply never make the same amount of money as men. But, it is as if they have an "I'll show you!" attitude and end up with nothing as soon as they can.

> *Trust in the* LORD WITH ALL YOUR HEART,
> *and do not lean on your own understanding.*
> *In all your ways acknowledge him,*
> *and he will make straight your paths.*
> Proverbs 3:5-6 ESV

• •

Jill was short and cute with a sparkly personality. She had a large circle of friends and was forever traveling. Jill was also an avid golfer and loved playing anytime she could get a foursome together.

Her divorce had occurred some years before I met her. She received a sizeable settlement and asked me for advice once we met, even though she had another broker at the time. Upon examining her portfolio, I discovered her current broker had placed margin trades in her account and she had a large margin balance. A margin account allows the client to borrow up to 50% of the value of their portfolio to purchase more stocks. The brokerage company charged a high-interest rate at that time on the funds borrowed. I do not agree with using margin accounts unless the client has a large portfolio and is knowledgeable about the risks involved when the markets decline. Jill was neither–she didn't have a clue. The broker was making more commission trades at her expense by using margin.

She asked me to manage her money. So I unwound her from the other brokerage company, paid off the margin debt by selling underperforming stocks and invested her remaining money in more conservative stocks without the added expense of margin interest.

I never asked what her original divorce settlement was but once she became my client, I soon discovered she was spending the money about as fast as she could. She would often call and say she needed several thousand dollars because she wanted to donate a large sum to a charity or she needed to help her family. She was never frivolous for herself. She drove a modest car, did not wear expensive jewelry, and dressed in a simple wardrobe. However, I later learned Jill never thought the money was hers, but considered the money her former husband's, and she wanted to get rid of it as soon as she could.

When she became my client, she was finishing her nursing degree and living in a small apartment. I encouraged her to buy a house for stability and the tax benefit. She thankfully took my advice, got a small mortgage and purchased a modest home in an older neighborhood.

Unfortunately, that did not stop the money drain. She continued to donate to every cause she heard of and to support her older brother–who although retired, should have been supporting himself. One day she called to ask for my advice about her brother. Over time, he accumulated a large credit card balance and he could not keep up with the payments. She wanted to pay it off. My question was, even though I didn't express it to her, how did her brother in his 70's manage to accumulate so much credit card debt? And, if she paid it off, what would stop him from doing it again?

I reminded her if she paid his debt, she would be out of money herself. I advised her not to pay his debt but to keep her money and grow it for her retirement. She said she would think about it.

Nevertheless, a few days later she called and asked me to liquidate her portfolio and send her the balance. She had blown through over $170,000 in less than 5 years that she had an account with me. Who knows how much she went through with the other broker she previously had. But, she successfully got rid of "her ex-husband's money"

ACTION POINTS:

- If you are divorced with a settlement from your ex-husband, consider that money **yours**–not **his**. A marriage involves two people's work, and the wife is entitled to the share she earned by raising children, working outside the home, managing the household, and her other contributions to the marriage. Jill was getting rid of ***her*** money, not his.

- The settlement may have been Jill's only opportunity to fund a comfortable retirement account for her future. By the time we met, she was approaching 50 and didn't have many more years to fund her retirement.

- Margin accounts are dangerous. Sure, you can own more stocks by using the ones you currently have as leverage (borrow the value to buy more). But what happens in a sudden market drop? You are required to sell stocks or come up with additional money to cover the margin debt. Most small investors should not be in this type of account. This leads to unnecessary buying and selling in the account (thereby creating more commission for your stockbroker) losses for the account holder and oftentimes, unnecessary taxes owed.

- Supporting financially inept relatives is the fastest way to end up with no money.

• •

Have you ever met a single woman–divorced or never married–who seemed to be "on hold"? She seems to be waiting for Mr. Right to come along or for her situation to change miraculously before she can begin her future life. She doesn't feel confident in making permanent decisions about where to live, where to work or what to do. She lives life looking around, scoping out the scene, judging everything and everyone through a narrow beam of "Is this the right one?" or "How will this work when I'm married?" or "When my life changes, I'll be fine."

Then, what happens when that moment of wedded bliss or change does not occur? Some women find themselves living a life that has no purpose, no structure, and no plan. A healthy life shouldn't be dependent upon another person or event that isn't even on the scene yet. Sadly, many single women find themselves in this position.

It ought to be the business of every day to prepare for our last day.
Matthew Henry

Dorothy loved playing the piano, driving fast, and eating spicy Thai or Mexican foods. She was a unique woman with short black hair and a masculine way of dressing–almost as though she was trying to deny her femininity. She often wore mannish hats that were her style trademark, but she was feminine otherwise and had a fun personality. She lived on the wild side. We met at a luncheon one day and soon became friends, probably because I liked Thai food too!

Divorced, she was the mother of three almost-grown children who lived with their father. She had not asked for custody of the children and they were happy to remain in the family home near their school and friends.

Later she told me why she divorced. She won a large settlement from a car accident, which gave her the financial means to leave her husband and unhappy marriage to begin a new life. She didn't ask her husband for a divorce settlement or alimony, since the divorce was her idea. She thought the accident settlement would be enough to support her until she could find a new husband. She was aggressive about finding men in the beginning and was especially bold. But the only ones she attracted were financially needy themselves or else not interested in marriage, so she was still alone.

Dorothy wasn't my client because we wanted to be friends rather than have a business relationship. Moreover, by the time we met, she didn't have much of her settlement left. She had bought and furnished a house, acquired a beautiful baby grand piano and a luxury automobile. She wasn't being a bit careful with her largesse because she was sure she would get remarried soon. She had also gone to a school to learn Holistic Therapy and was trying to build a clientele of patients but she had not been very successful.

Then she reasoned that if she had an attractive office, she might attract more clients. So, she leased a private office, furnished it, and spent many dollars in rent. But that didn't improve her clientele count and she had to give up the space and move out. She spent a great deal in rent, on décor, and office furnishings that she couldn't recover. Of course, she neglected to do a market survey or talk to any other therapists–she barged ahead without a firm plan.

Having met some realtors near her office, she determined that her next career move would be the real estate business. She studied and passed the real estate exam, associated with a realtor, and began trying to sell real estate. I even gave her the listing for a house I was going to sell, but she couldn't find any buyers and there were few showings. She failed in that career as well.

Running out of options, she decided to sell her house and move to a larger city where she bought another house closer to her brother and father. Her father, who was in a nursing home, had a large estate, and Dorothy's brother was managing it. They decided that Dorothy would further her college education by studying nursing but, she was unable to pass the difficult medical classes. Then she settled on psychology and that took her about two years to earn an associate's degree in family counseling.

With her brother paying for her education and living expenses through her father's estate, she was able to afford her daily life. The plan was to secure a job in her new chosen field and again become self-sufficient. She obtained a position with a small counseling office; but, the position did not last long. She told me the program was discontinued and maybe it was, but she didn't ever go back to work in that field. I'm not sure she ever went back to work at all. We lost touch after that.

Dorothy was someone who blew through her large settlement of money and never looked back. Over the years of our friendship, I offered to look at her portfolio at no charge and no obligation, but she declined. From several things she said, she was invested in stocks and also on margin, and suffered large losses because of that. Her broker called her often and recommended she buy or sell stocks but she had no concept what she was agreeing to. The broker was the only one making money buying and selling stocks for her because her balance kept going down.

I offered her suggestions from time to time about budgeting and being careful, but she would laugh them off. I believe she knew her brother wouldn't let her starve, so she simply proceeded to spend and live life as though there was a never-ending supply of money, which, I guess, in essence, there was because of her brother's management of their father's estate.

Dorothy was pretty, lively, talented, and intelligent–but she didn't care about her future enough to be practical or careful. Once or twice, she would date someone but no relationship ever blossomed. As the years passed, she stopped even looking for someone to help support her since her brother had taken on that role. She regretted divorcing her husband, but he had remarried so that door closed.

She blew through several hundred thousand dollars without a backward glance and ended up with no money and no future. It was such a waste. If she had been wise and cautiously invested her money, lived within a budget, and chosen a profitable career path, she could have been a success. She had the intelligence and basic survival skills needed; she didn't have the discipline or desire. She was content to let her husband and later her brother take care of her.

ACTION POINTS:

- Dorothy didn't set out to spend all her money recklessly, but she succeeded just the same. She bought too many items immediately, such as a house, car, piano, furniture–without knowing how she was going to support herself. She would have been smarter to rent an apartment and buy those items once she was successful and making money.

- Again, she had a stockbroker who was more interested in making money for him than for her. She didn't understand what he was doing and wouldn't ask anyone for help. She was a very independent and rebellious woman who would not take anyone's advice about anything. That is never a good attitude to have.

- She entered into new careers without doing much research, spent money on office space and décor for a business that was failing, and jumped from one failure to another without trying to determine what was causing all her defeats. She would never ask experts in the field for advice but continued to bleed money that she couldn't afford to lose.

> *"The wise woman builds her house,*
> *but with her own hands the foolish one tears hers down*
> Proverbs 14:1 NIV

• •

I first met Candis at a women's social group where I spoke about finances. She came up to me after my talk and asked for a business card saying she might need help with her finances. We visited a few moments and I invited her to call and schedule an appointment. She called me shortly after that and inquired about my services and we arranged a time to meet.

At our first meeting, she arrived with a flourish–dressed in stylish clothes and adorned with expensive jewelry. Candis was blond, in good physical shape since she played tennis and had a witty personality. She gave the appearance of someone who was raised with money.

During my fact-finding interview, I discovered she was recently divorced and quite bitter towards her ex-husband. They had enjoyed a rich lifestyle in another, larger city until the economy started to lag with one of the oil busts that Texas regularly 'enjoys'. Candis' position as an engineer no longer existed and she was unemployed.

She and her husband had no children, so when the marriage began failing, she secured an attorney and began fighting for a good settlement and custody of their four Golden retrievers. Her husband fought back for custody of the four dogs, not because he cared that much about them, but for advantage. The final decree issued after a long, bitter struggle awarded two dogs to each of them. She also received a healthy financial settlement, which came from dividing their community property and assets.

The settlement should have been more than sufficient to support her, except for the fact that she could not bear the thought that her husband had two of the dogs and she was certain he wouldn't treat them well. She also believed the two dogs she was awarded were grieving and missing his two dogs. So, she filed a lawsuit to recover the other two dogs and have them placed in her custody. This involved attorney fees, meetings, and negotiations that finally ended with Candis paying her ex-husband over $40,000 to gain custody of the two dogs and paying both his and her attorney fees. Only then was Candis satisfied.

By this time, she had purchased a home and moved her possessions over 200 miles using a professional moving company who packed and unpacked her at a substantial cost. Once when I visited her home I was introduced to the menagerie she housed–birds and other little caged critters, and of course the four Golden retrievers. This vast collection cost her considerable money in feed and vet bills, but she did not care. Animals were her children and husband.

This had all transpired in her life before we met and she became my client. Naturally, she thought to invest with me would enable her to recover the vast amounts of money she had already lost to attorney fees for reclaiming the two dogs, purchasing the new house, and her spendthrift lifestyle of partying and entertaining. I explained to her that I didn't invest my clients in a 'get rich quick' way and that I would place her in somewhat conservative stocks and mutual funds which would give her a sense of security and not lose a lot of value in market dips. She agreed at that point but I soon found she expected much more.

She realized she would need an income and could not continue her lifestyle living on her remaining divorce settlement. So, she decided to enroll in a local college to become a paralegal since she had no other marketable skills. She kept somewhat busy with her studies; however, she would call me often for advances from her account because she needed more money to support her lifestyle. Her account balances were dropping and not because of the markets. Of course, she was not happy with me. I tried explaining to her that I couldn't work miracles, but she wasn't convinced.

After a while, she completed enough of her degree process to be ready for job interviews. She was excited to be reaching the point where she could be earning money again. But, she immediately hated the job-hunting experience. She would regale me with stories of the firms she interviewed with, how she wasn't treated with the respect of her education and financial standing and how she was expected to begin working at the lowest level available. She was miserable. Not just with the poor job opportunities available, but with her life in general. Of course, she wasn't happy with my money-management either since her account balance could not keep up with her extravagant lifestyle.

Once more, she put out some feelers to her old profession and found there was a job available in her former field in another city. She made a visit and secured the job–she was thrilled! As soon as she could, she purchased a new house in an expensive area in the new city–and the movers called again to pack and move her belongings. Off she went, but with a lot, less money than she brought with her. After a few months in the new city, she called to tell me she was moving her account to another broker with another firm. I will give her credit–at least she told me upfront rather than having her new broker transfer it without warning. I did not hear from her again and often wondered how she fared.

Candis was probably able to recover sufficiently if she maintained her new position. If she had secured a paralegal position with her lavish lifestyle, she would have gone through her divorce settlement very quickly. She wasn't willing to listen to reason or live within her budget. She was very fortunate to get a second chance.

ACTION POINTS:

- Candis spent money after her divorce that she should not have spent. Since she was re-tooling a career, she should have tried to adjust her lifestyle and not continue to live as if there was plenty of money in her account.

- She should have thoroughly researched the career she thought she wanted, rather than moving from her original town, going back to school–only to discover she didn't like the new town or the new career she had chosen. She could have met with various women in the paralegal field and judged their lifestyle, their working conditions, and their opinions about the field before making the mistakes she did.

- Spending so much money going back to court to regain custody of the two dogs was extravagant and a move she couldn't afford. If she had to have the dogs, she should have made every effort to win that custody battle along with the divorce.

CHAPTER FOUR

KNOWLEDGE IS GOLD

....

If you are nearing retirement, have absolutely no knowledge of what to do about your retirement plan, and don't understand taxes, **PLEASE** consult with two or more advisors before making any withdrawals or retiring. Please do this **BEFORE** you reach the age when you must begin Required Minimum Distributions. This is imperative! Huge mistakes are being made daily by people who are retiring and don't know the ramifications of that decision–not only to their retirement plans, but on claiming their Social Security, beginning Medicare, and income taxes.

For the Lord gives wisdom;
from his mouth come knowledge and understanding;
Proverbs 2:6 NIV

I received a surprise email one morning stating the following: *"It has been awhile since I got your email from my friend Sandra. I have a question for you. My husband just draw out his 401k fund about 390 thousand after paid 95 thousand tax, because he is 72 years old. San-*

dra said ask you to see if you want to manage it for him. If you do what fund plan. Please let me know. Thank you."

The email above is copied exactly as I received it. This couple was from Asia and had been in the US for many years. But, the email doesn't convey a good command of the English language nor does it show any financial expertise. Sadly, Nguyen Liang had retired and agreed to take out his entire 401(k) balance. According to IRS rules, a 20% tax must be withheld on the amount withdrawn. He did not first consult a tax advisor and had no idea what he was doing.

I got on the telephone and began asking him and his wife questions. Neither understood that he had other options. He simply thought since he was retiring, he had to take out all his money and leave his company. Neither was aware of what the addition of over $471,000 of income would do to their tax situation for that year. And, neither had any idea what to do going forward. That is why his wife emailed me, thanks to another client giving them my name.

His withdrawal of the 401(k) money had occurred in March about 3 weeks before they contacted me. I first called his employer to get the plan details (he gave them permission to talk to me) and I received a photocopy of the final paperwork. The best solution would have been to put the money back into the 401(k) plan and withdraw it properly, but that was not possible. The plan had already sent him the money and had withheld about $93,000 in Federal Withholding. The transaction could not be redone or canceled.

As luck would have it, we were still within the 60-day non-taxable rollover period, which would allow Mr. Liang to roll over the 401(k) distribution into an IRA and save the tax, but we had to move fast. More problematic, I had to try to convey the facts and figures to Mr. and Mrs. Liang, bridge the language barrier, and show them what the advantage would be. That was a difficult task, but we finally managed. When I told them they could save money, at least they were eager to discover how.

Without getting too technical, Mr. Liang had to come up with the rollover eligible amount, which was the $471,000 less his Required Minimum Distribution for the current year of a little over $18,000, or $453,000. He had received a check for $378,800 from his plan, so he needed to come up with approximately $74,200 to bring his balance up to $453,000, the amount that was eligible for rollover to save him the tax. Thankfully, he had no problem coming up with the $74,200 so the rollover could proceed.

I proposed a variable annuity for the bulk of the money, which would provide him with a guaranteed death benefit of the amount deposited less any withdrawals and a guaranteed 5% withdrawal for life with spouse continuation. If the annuity increased in value, the gains would lock-in each year. This would give him the guarantees in a down market that stock and bond investments would not have. He could take his annual Required Minimum Distribution from the annuity each year or even in monthly checks. His wife could continue the plan if he died. If they both died, the remaining amount would go to their beneficiaries. It was an easy solution for them that took care of him, his wife, and later, his children.

For the remaining money, I proposed a managed stock account comprised of conservative stocks to provide growth.

When the Liang's did their taxes the next year, they were able to claim as a refund nearly all of the $93,000 tax previously paid except for the tax due on the annual Required Minimum Distribution he had taken the previous March–or a refund of approximately $88,900. They were very happy with that sized tax refund.

Over the years, his annuity performed very well because of its guarantees. Better than the managed stock account because the stock market collapsed due to the failures of large financial institutions in September 2008, which ultimately caused an economic crisis in other countries around the world. It was quite a while before that account recovered, but the bulk of his money was in the annuity and growing each year.

I always counseled my clients never to pay the IRS taxes until they were due. In Mr. Liang's case, he would have paid the full amount upfront on his 401(k) withdrawal. There were other ways of delaying the payment of those taxes. Receiving all this retirement money in one year meant he would have paid an unnecessary amount of income tax in that year. Then if he had invested the money or even put it into a savings account, he would have paid taxes on the earned income each year. Instead, by doing the rollover, he saved $88,900, and then his investments were tax-deferred except for the tax on his annual Required Minimum Distribution.

It pays to have some tax knowledge or at least be associated with someone who does.

ACTION POINTS:

- Everyone should make a written retirement plan:

    o When am I going to retire from my job?
    o What am I going to do with the money I have saved in my company retirement plan?
    o Can I roll over that amount into my individual retirement account (IRA)? If so, how will I invest that money?
    o When can I begin taking Social Security?
    o What are the tax implications of these moves?

· ·

When you fall in love, whether you're young or older, be careful. Be especially wary if it's with someone from a different culture or country. Sure, the accent is urbane; their stories are different from any you've ever heard, they're sophisticated it seems–nothing like your friends or other people you've dated. Their customs are different, their belief system is different, and they may indulge you in ways you've only dreamed of. However, not all that glitters is gold.

43

> *The plans of the diligent lead surely to abundance,*
> *but everyone who is hasty comes only to poverty.*
> Proverbs 21:5 ESV

When I first met Katherine, she was a newlywed. Her husband was a chef at a local well-known hotel and she was head over heels in love and awe of such an accomplished man. Besides, he was a charming European and had swept her off her feet. She simply bubbled as she talked about him.

I had given a talk about finances at a local women's group where she attended, so she talked to me afterward and wondered if I could help her with an inheritance, she had recently received when her mother died. It wasn't a considerable sum, but she wasn't sure what to do with it.

We scheduled an appointment to go over the paperwork and I learned that the money was still invested in mutual funds her mother had chosen during her lifetime. Some were good funds and some not so good, so I made some recommendations for changes and Katherine agreed, becoming my client.

Katherine was born and raised in South Dakota in a modest, mid-western family. She had known many second or third-generation Europeans since they settled in her town over the years. When she met her future husband, who was a chef at a local hotel and came from Europe, she thought they had a lot in common. Katherine had two married sisters who settled in two different states, but she was unmarried and alone. She couldn't wait to say "Yes!" when Josef asked her to wed.

She had been my client for a few years, when she called one day all excited to tell me she and her husband were going to move to France where he had an opportunity to join another chef in opening a restaurant in a large city. She was thrilled for the adventure but also apprehensive about leaving her family. By this time, she had birthed their first child–a son. She was feeling a little nervous to be so far away in a country where she didn't know the language and knew no one except her husband, but she told me her in-laws were there and would be a big help to her.

We first had to figure out what to do about her financial portfolio. After much wrangling with my back office, I was able to maintain her account in the US even though she had a foreign address. That was a relief to her, since she planned to visit her sisters in the US from time to time and wanted to have US dollars to spend while here rather than Euros since the exchange rate was more favorable here.

So, Katherine, her husband, and son moved to France and she began to adapt to European life. They lived in a small apartment at first, which wasn't to her liking, but she adjusted. Her husband worked long hours almost 7 days a week since he was the head chef and joint owner of a struggling new restaurant which left her alone with their little son hours on end.

She made several trips to the US to visit her sisters and I always arranged to have a check sent to a sister, which Katherine could cash and spend while visiting. That arrangement worked out well. It was handy for her to have money here rather than having to get it exchanged in France before she left.

A new baby arrived after they had been in France for a few years–a little girl this time. Katherine would call me on occasion to inquire about her money and would infer vaguely that not all was rosy in her life. Her in-laws were being intrusive and wanted to dictate how the children were to be raised and educated. Her husband agreed with his parents. Poor Katherine had no one to turn to except her sisters a continent and ocean away.

Then, she began calling to say 'they' needed money because the business wasn't going so well and that began draining her account. Another time she told me she could not bring the children with her to visit because her husband forbade it. At that time, a spouse had to give signed permission for juveniles to leave the country with only

45

one spouse, and he would not sign the papers. I'm sure their marriage was very strained at that point and he was fearful she would take the children to the US and not come back.

I had been filing a non-resident tax return for them over the years to report the dividends received on her account so if she ever returned to the US, it would be easier to pick up where she left off with the IRS. They didn't have to pay any tax, but it did report the gains and losses on her investments. At last, when she realized she wasn't going to have any money left and couldn't return to the US, she told me not to bother filing the tax form any longer.

Finally, one day she called and asked me to close her account and have a check sent to her for the balance–her husband needed the money for his business. Her voice was flat and tired–she had at length resigned to the fact that she was without any assets to her name and her prince charming was not a prince anymore. I felt sorry for her. She had been such a bubbly and happy person looking forward to a storybook life. Now all she had were the ashes of what had been.

She told me if I ever traveled to France, to look her up and she would have a room for me. I know she would have and it would have been great to see her again. I've thought of her often and wondered whatever happened to her life that began with such promise. I know she never thought she would end up a virtual captive in a foreign land, penniless, and at her husband's mercy.

ACTION PLANS:

- It is needless to say; Katherine should have arranged her life differently and not allowed her new husband to completely devastate her life and her financial security.

- Katherine should have suspected that a change in countries, languages, and family dynamics with in-laws involved might lead to problems.

- Since her money was in her name alone, it would have been possible for her to refuse to allow her husband access to it, but that would have caused additional problems for her, I'm sure.

- A reminder, that love does not conquer all.

CHAPTER FIVE

PLANNING IS KEY

. . . .

An adage: *"People don't plan to fail–they simply fail to plan"*. This is true, especially for people who are going into business for themselves. They should have a business plan before they ever begin. There are numerous examples on the internet and before that, there were many books written on how to begin a business. SCORE is available for free coaching and mentoring by retired entrepreneurs through the Small Business Administration. If a person will take the time to make a business plan, evaluate it carefully and allow an expert to critique it, they will save time and money and find the expertise they need.

> *But those who desire to be rich fall into temptation, into a snare, into many senseless and harmful desires that plunge people into ruin and destruction."*
> 1 Timothy 6:9 ESV

Sharon called me one day to inquire about her husband's life insurance policies. I had not written these policies on George, but had become the agent assigned to them, so I hadn't yet met Sharon and George.

The policies were old and weren't keeping up with his needs to provide coverage for his family. I asked Sharon if he was in good health and he was, so I proposed a term policy with a much larger death benefit. She talked it over with George, and they decided that would be the best way to go. He filled out an application, took the required health exam, and became approved–so we began our relationship with a $1million term insurance policy.

About two years later, I received a call from George. The company he worked for had sold and since he had an ESOP (Employee Stock Ownership Plan) worth quite a bit of money, he decided to take the money and pay the tax rather than roll it over into a tax-deferred retirement account. I questioned the logic of that decision because of the large tax bill he would have to pay. But, he said he had always dreamed of being his own boss and wanted to buy a ranch and start raising cattle. He had thought it through and that was his final decision. There was no changing his mind.

Sharon and George wanted to meet with me and discuss how I would propose investing the money they would have left after buying the ranch. They wanted to grow it over the years for their retirement. At the time George was around 45, so he would have about 20 years to grow the money. If everything worked as planned, he could have his new enterprise plus a solid retirement account when he needed it.

So, after several meetings, we decided upon a managed account of stocks and bonds. Additionally, they each had small IRA accounts, which we left in mutual funds.

George found a 250-acre ranch and purchased it for cash along with a few head of cattle. He was overjoyed. They maintained their older home in town and seemed content with their new endeavor.

But soon, they began talking about building a small ranch house on the acreage and selling their home in town. As the house plans began to unfold, it was no longer going to be a modest ranch house. It had morphed into a large, sprawling home–which was lovely, but cost more and more as the construction proceeded. Of course, they were going to need part of their money to do this, so I liquidated stock several times to cover the construction costs.

Sharon and I met for lunch one day and she told me about the people they now knew. All were wealthy ranchers and had been for years. George was beginning to build a head of registered cattle. They were also planning to purchase and raise emus because the meat was so healthy and there was a big demand for it in health food circles. They were going to use the income from their cattle and emu business to pay back the money they took from their investment accounts to build the house.

I wasn't an expert in cattle or emus, but I could guess from the sound of events they were attending and the people they were associating with, they were probably in over their heads financially and socially.

Not long afterward, Sharon called to tell me she was opening a small retail boutique in an exclusive strip mall. The shop would sell Western wear and handcrafted silver jewelry from various silversmiths out west. She needed another withdrawal from their account to stock the inventory.

With all the withdrawals, their account wouldn't be able to sustain them in retirement. I mentioned this to her, but she brushed it off saying "That's a long way in the future".

Now we were entering the Obama years when the stock market had several hiccups and the health insurance industry was in disarray. Sharon and George were older now and both had developed some serious health problems. Moreover, their health insurance premiums were extraordinarily expensive, so every few years they would shop for a cheaper plan and rate. But now the new plans wouldn't cover their pre-existing conditions. Then too, the emu business had failed because the meat was no longer a fad. Everyone had their emus for sale with no buyers. If that weren't enough, Sharon's boutique was not making expenses of rent and utilities, so she had to liquidate and take the losses.

Of course, there were frequent calls for money out of their account to pay taxes, pay insurance, or merely to keep afloat. At last, they called to liquidate the remainder of the account. They were sorry and so was I.

They had begun with such high hopes. But poor management of their lifestyle, not researching the pros and cons of the cattle, emu, and boutique business–meant their investment was gone. So was their dream of a carefree retirement.

ACTION PLANS:

- Removing all the money from the ESOP plan and paying the taxes due to pursue a dream without prior planning is usually a recipe for failure.

- When trying to 'keep up with the Jones' many people fall into financial ruin. Before purchasing the ranch, they were not socializing with moneyed people. They did not have the social expertise or the money to keep up.

- Beginning a new business of raising exotic birds was risky. This was something he had no experience doing. The same was true with the registered cattle

- Opening a boutique was also risky. Neither had any experience running a retail establishment.

- Health insurance costs were exorbitant. They could have changed this scenario by securing employment under a company plan as an employee. Neither Sharon nor George wanted to get a job and become an employee of another company to receive this benefit so they were at the mercy of insurance companies.

> *Whoever loves money never has enough: whoever loves wealth is never satisfied with their income. This too is meaningless*
> Ecclesiastes 5:10 NIV

. . . .

Occasionally a client would be the type that I had to "tip-toe" around to keep from upsetting them. I would find myself evaluating everything I said and did because they would immediately challenge my position and I would have to defend myself. I was raised with a few people like that, so I was experienced in accommodating those personalities. It was not always easy for me, but I knew the client's history was the contributor and it was not my responsibility to change them.

When I was still giving monthly seminars, Freida attended one and immediately requested an appointment with me at my office.

She had a portfolio with a local broker in town but she needed more monthly income. He had positioned her money in a series of bonds and stocks that weren't performing well enough to provide her with the income she needed or wanted. I suggested several changes to her portfolio that would increase her monthly income while giving her a sense of security in a down market. She was ecstatic and wanted me to become her broker immediately.

Widowed for many years when we met, her deceased husband had been a professional and their lives were quite prosperous. Unfortunately, the money he left at death wasn't enough for Freida to cover the lifestyle she chose to maintain. She had a modest home that was attractively furnished and decorated and she had a renter named Sam who lived in her house. She did his laundry and provided his meals but he had his separate bedroom. They went everywhere together and most people considered them a 'couple' since they had been together for many years. But Freida kept the appearances of being single for estate purposes, or so she said.

As I came to know Freida, she began to tell me more about her family background. She was born in Germany before WW2 and her parents sent her to America as a child of twelve to escape the Holocaust. Her family was Jewish and the persecution of her parents had already begun when she left. Freida traveled on a train and then a ship for passage to the US–all arranged and funded by various Jewish women's organizations. A Jewish family in Texas agreed to foster her in their home once she arrived.

She proceeded to learn English and receive her education. She then graduated from college and later married her husband. Determined not to have a foreign accent, she practiced speaking until she had no trace of one. Back in Germany, her parents and siblings perished in the Holocaust, but it took her years to find out where and how. She had many emotions to deal with and never fully succeeded in making peace with her past. She had an enormous case of survivor's guilt.

She was a study in stylish flamboyance–bleached blond hair, heavy make-up, bright red manicured nails, diamond rings, and expensive, heavy necklaces with earrings to match. When she dressed to go out, she was impeccable and chose from her vast wardrobe of elegant clothes. She drove a huge Lincoln, shopped in the finest local boutiques, and regularly went to other cities to browse and look for bargains.

When she was at home, she wore colorful caftans while cooking or lounging. Her home contained collectible glassware, art pieces, and expensive décor. She also had numerous sets of china and silver because she loved to entertain and would have large dinner parties to celebrate Jewish holidays or other events. Sam was an avid angler and kept her table supplied with fresh fish or soft-shelled crabs. She was an extraordinary cook and her meals were always an event with her encouraging everyone to have more, more, more. After dinner as she would plop down on the couch her favorite statement was, "Oh, my fat hurts!"

But, she was very demanding of her friends and me. She expected me to be available to come to her home whenever she had a question with the promise to reward my efforts with dinner or a special dessert. This always resulted in a lovely meal, but I didn't dare risk turning down an invitation or she would be upset.

Over time, I was able to position her portfolio with annuities that gave her a guaranteed monthly withdrawal. As the annuities grew in value, we would roll them into a newer one with better guarantees and increase her monthly income. She was always happy to have more money to spend. We didn't touch one annuity, however, because it was an excellent contract and I didn't want to roll it over into a new one. She agreed.

She had been my client for about 10 years, when I had to move back to my hometown to care for my elderly mother in her final days. All my clients remained with me as I made this move and we were all able to remain in touch through phone calls and mail. I also made annual visits to each client.

After I had been gone about a year, Freida called and requested I send her portfolio information to her new insurance agent–"a really nice young man who lived not too far away." He had become her homeowners' insurance rep. She also told me of how many times he had been by to eat and how much he enjoyed her cooking. Of course, I had to agree to do this, but I warned her not to change anything because it would cost her money and ruin the plan we had in place. Nevertheless, I knew she would be moving her account because he was her 'new favorite person'.

Sure enough, in a very short time, I received notice that her account transferred to this new agent, and Freida did not even bother to call and let me know. I visited her later when I was in the area–just as a friendly visit. I didn't mention her accounts and neither did she. I can only hope he handled her investments well. I also hope he paid proper attention to her because if he didn't–she would leave him for the next one who did. Sadly, anyone who wanted to be her friend had to lavish her with attention. The same applied to anyone who wanted to do business with her it turned out.

ACTION POINTS:

- Live within your means. Freida always wanted more than what her money allowed. She didn't care what safety measures were in a product but only in the amount of monthly income it would provide so she would have more to spend.

- She was desperate for the approval of others and thereby charmed people so they would be her friend. She needed people around her that would make her feel wanted and important. But if she found someone else who provided her with more attention, she dismissed her older friends who were now considered inadequate. She recounted numerous stories to me of this behavior in her past, so I was not surprised–only disappointed. That is not how you choose and retain professional people in your life. They are not in business to accommodate your personality disorders.

CHAPTER SIX

FAMILY DEALINGS: A STUDY IN RELATIONSHIPS

....

One of my hobbies is genealogy. It is always interesting to meet siblings in a family and study their facial features and lifestyles to see if they match. Sometimes, I find siblings who seem to have no commonalities at all. What type of childhood formed their adult lifestyles? How could they come from the same family and yet be so completely different? Bill and Eliza were this type of brother and sister.

When I began working at a large brokerage firm, to secure new clients, I held afternoon 'dessert seminars' at a nearby cafeteria. It worked well, because the cafeteria wasn't busy around 2:00 PM, the attendees could choose their favorite dessert along with a beverage, and we were given a private room in which to meet. I acquired many new clients that way.

Bill was one of those clients. He was a short, wiry fellow with a full head of wavy gray hair. He paid rapt attention to my presentation as well as the CPA who gave tax pointers. Afterward, he signed a card that he was interested in an appointment.

In a few days, we had a meeting at my office. He was quite an interesting fellow having a background as a trumpet player in some of the big bands that played in Las Vegas. He was full of interesting stories of the musicians and famous singers he had known years before. Of course, Bill hadn't played Vegas for many years but he had a sharp memory.

His financial plan was in disarray, if it had ever been a plan. He didn't have a lot of money and was concerned that what he did have was dwindling due to a lack of management. He didn't have a financial advisor but did have some mutual funds that he had owned for years. Some were stocks funds, the others were bonds funds, and both were showing losses. He wanted more monthly income, but was not able to get it from the mutual funds he had.

I suggested government-backed mortgage bonds–which paid monthly income and were tax efficient. He agreed that would be a good plan for him–so he became my client.

He followed me as a client after I left the large brokerage firm and affiliated with an independent broker-dealer. I needed new paperwork signed, so he asked if I could come to his apartment rather than him coming to my office and I agreed. His apartment was in a nice area and building, but his unit was neglected and dirty, especially since he shared occupancy with several cats, which always make me sneeze. It was readily apparent that Bill drank often and was a chain-smoker. I could smell the liquor on his breath at a distance and the apartment was blue with smoke. I did not linger any longer than necessary.

We continued to do business and stay in touch by telephone. A little over a year later, I received a call from his sister, Eliza, telling me that Bill had fallen and she was moving him to an assisted living facility not far from where she lived in another town. She said she was at his apartment getting things cleared out and asked if I could meet her there the next day. I agreed.

When we met, I was pleasantly surprised. She was nothing like Bill, except she was also a musician. A church organist. She was friendly and I could tell she wasn't a drinker or a smoker. She asked me a few questions about myself and asked how Bill and I met. She had found statements from his account with me and had a few questions about them. She had his Power of Attorney, so we could discuss his finances with no qualms. I could tell she was hesitant and careful in her questions, but as we talked, she seemed to relax. By the time I was ready to leave, she was smiling. She gave me the address of the assisted living facility where Bill was going to live and we parted ways.

Sometime after that, Bill called to give me his ex-wife's name. He said I should call her because she needed help with her money the same as he did. Loraine became my client too, which I'll write about below.

About a year later because Bill's government bonds were not performing as well as they had been, I called and suggested to him that he make some changes in his account. He thought that was a great idea, so I drove to the assisted living facility where he lived.

We had a fun visit and I was surprised he still had cats in his room—and even on his bed. While I was trying to explain the investments to him that I was proposing, he seemed to be fidgety and in a hurry. Not knowing why, I asked and he said it was time for his cigarette and he didn't want to miss it. I told him I'd wait, so he wheeled out of his room and down the hall into another small room where there was a small group of people gathered. They shut the door and an aide proceeded to light everyone's cigarettes. As I watched through a hallway window, the room soon filled with smoke with everyone puffing away as fast as they could. Once finished smoking, everyone came out. Then, Bill and I were able to finish our business conversation with the cats as witnesses. He happily informed me he could have an alcoholic drink every evening with his dinner. Just like home!

Bill was in that facility for about 2 years before his death and he didn't run out of money, cigarettes, or booze. Plus, he and his cats were happy. He was 79 when he died.

ACTION POINTS:

- Bill was fortunate he had any money left given his lifestyle of alcoholism and not paying any attention to his investments.

- I never recommended Long Term Care Insurance for nursing homes, and Bill's experience proves that few people ever need that coverage.

- Bill never questioned the investments I made for him nor made any effort to comprehend what they were. That is dangerous for a client, but it was more often the case than not.

· ·

LORAINE

Bill's ex-wife, Loraine, lived in a city to the north of my office. She was expecting my call because Bill told her I managed his money so she should have me manage hers too.

We met at her condominium, which was in a lovely high-rise building. When I entered, I was pleasantly surprised at how beautifully decorated it was. There were floor to ceiling mirrors on most of the walls. Her furniture was French provincial, carpets were lush and the décor was very tasteful and expensive.

Loraine was a tiny, delicate woman with a soft voice, expressive hands, and beautiful jewelry that she wore without pretense. Her hair was professionally styled and her clothes appeared expensive and well-fitted to her tiny frame. Sitting on her sofa, she reminded me of a little china doll in a museum.

She was 73 when we met and she had the same eclectic collection of mutual funds that Bill had previously owned. Bill had told her what changes he made and she was interested in changing her portfolio to the same-type investments.

While visiting, she told me they were still close, although divorced, but that they just couldn't live together. She had written and published a few little books and had worked as a professional singer in Las Vegas for many years. That is how they met. They were married for quite a number of years but had no children.

Loraine needed monthly income since her expenses continued to increase. She had a caregiver come each day to clean and cook for her, and to drive her to doctor appointments, and buy groceries. The current woman had been with her for a while, but there had been various others in the past. Loraine ruefully told me some were honest and some were not.

The expenses on her condominium continued to rise and her car was getting older and requiring more repairs. However, she was determined to remain where she was if possible.

She had a small IRA and another non-retirement account with a total net worth of about $260,000 not counting her condominium. We agreed on a portfolio that was a combination of government mortgage bonds and income-producing mutual funds–which suited her needs.

In the five years she was my client, she would call from time to time and ask for a withdrawal–usually around $2000 - $3000. The last year before her death, she, like Bill, went into an assisted living facility and she would call sometimes and ask for a larger sum of money. She was only there about six months before her death at age 80.

Since neither Bill nor Loraine had children, Loraine named her niece as her beneficiary. After Loraine's death, the niece contacted me and she had no hesitation liquidating her aunt's account as soon as she could.

ACTION POINTS:

- Loraine had done a good job of managing her lifestyle and living within her monthly income.

- Loraine, like her ex-husband Bill, never understood the investments she had. I explained the ones I made for her, but she just waved it off as unimportant. She didn't want to bother trying to understand but wanted to rely on me to make the decisions. That made my life easier, but if I had been trying to steal her money, it would have been quite easy.

- Like Bill, Loraine went into an assisted living facility and did not need any additional money than what she had.

> *Command those who are rich in this present world not to be arrogant nor to put their hope in wealth, which is so uncertain, but to put their hope in God, who richly provides us with everything for our enjoyment. Command them to do good, to be rich in good deeds, and to be generous and willing to share. In this way they will lay up treasure for themselves as a firm foundation for the coming age, so that they may take hold of the life that is truly life*
>
> 1 Timothy 6:17-19 NIV

....

ELIZA AND HUSBAND JOHN

Eliza, of course, was Bill's sister. We kept in touch after our brief meeting before Bill went into the assisted living near her.

She called me about Bill's taxes one spring when she discovered he had not taken his Required Minimum Distribution from his IRA and she had no idea what to do. The IRS can impose a harsh penalty of up to 50% of the RMD amount on taxpayers that fail to take their distributions. I asked her to send me his paperwork. The IRS requires their specific Power of Attorney, so I asked her to procure that with Bill's signature permitting me to contact the IRS on his behalf. I wrote the IRS a letter explaining that Bill was in an assisted living facility, was elderly, and had mistakenly missed the RMD. They responded that all he had to do was file an amended return, take out the RMD, and pay the taxes due on the amended return. Eliza was thrilled to know everything had been handled so easily.

When Bill died, Eliza was his beneficiary on the accounts he had with me. I called to express my condolences and she asked if she and her husband, John, could schedule a meeting with me. Of course! They suggested a nice restaurant for lunch and so began a fascinating relationship.

Both Eliza and John were musicians. She was a professional piano accompanist and organist while they both performed vocal music in churches and for civic groups. Eliza taught music in public school while John was a college professor. They had no children and were completely devoted to a collection of nieces and nephews scattered around the country. They were also faithful members and musical participants in their church. Since I also had a history of vocal music and love of performance, we had many common interests.

Eliza then confided that before she met me, she was prepared to think I was only after her brother's money and she had requested we meet that day at his apartment to dismiss me. But, after meeting and talking to me, she realized I wasn't that type of person and now they wanted to talk to me about managing their money! What a lovely surprise! She had also talked to Loraine and knew she was happy with the service I provided. I was happy to have them as clients.

Eliza was a cancer survivor and in good health. However, John had numerous health problems so when we met they were in the process of moving to a larger town so he would be closer to good hospitals. It was a hard move for them since they had a large circle of friends in the smaller town where they had lived for years. Both were very out-going and friendly, so it wasn't long before they had a new church home and a large circle of friends in the college town where they moved.

Both had sizeable teacher retirement accounts and other assets, so they were looking for some growth of principle plus monthly income. At the time we met, 911 had caused havoc with the markets and the country was still struggling to get financial footing. I didn't want to use mutual funds nor did I want to suggest bonds because interest rates and the stock market were not predictable. Therefore, we chose annuities since they were offering annual guarantees by locking in growth, and clients could take a monthly income that would not disturb the contract benefits.

We made the transfers into the annuities and John and Eliza were happy with the results. When we met, the subject of income taxes came up. John wanted to know if their new investments would cause any changes in their taxable income–the answer was no. Then John asked me about doing their taxes, which I agreed to do.

Everything was calm for the next few years–the annuities were performing well and I was doing their income taxes each year. Then in mid-2007 John called me and said he had gotten a letter from the IRS stating he owed them over $8000 on their 2005 income taxes and he had 30 days to pay it. Should he send them a check? "No, no, no!" I said, "Send me a copy of their letter and let me see what's happened."

The year 2005 had been an unusual year that allowed taxpayers to donate larger than normal gifts to charitable organizations after August 27, 2005, and not have the 50% of income limitations apply. John and Eliza had exceeded the usual 50% limit on purpose because they wanted to make a substantial gift to their church so they timed it to be after August 27, 2005. Nevertheless, for whatever reason, the IRS had disallowed their entire charitable contribution amount instead of following their own rules and sent them a bill for over $8000.

I was thankful John called me before he wrote the check–otherwise, he was ready to send them what they asked for. The IRS is not always correct; in fact, over the years I've found they are often incorrect. After a series of letters to the IRS providing even more proof of their charitable deductions and dates when they were given, the IRS allowed the total amount claimed and considered the matter closed. So, I was again considered their hero!

One memory I love about John and Eliza: once when I was visiting them at their condominium, I arrived as scheduled and John met me at the door. He said, "Eliza's not here right now. She's interviewing a cat." Did my ears hear right? Sure enough! She had the same love for cats that Bill, her brother, had and she was looking for a new one. I didn't know people interviewed cats, but Eliza certainly did.

Sadly, Eliza died of pancreatic cancer in 2010 and her death was swift. John was devastated because they always presumed he would be the first to die since his health was so precarious. He lived on for another 5 years, dying at age 85.

John and Eliza were a happy couple very much in love with each other. They made it a point to be active members and deeply involved with their church and other organizations plus they enjoyed a wide circle of friends. Both were interesting conversationalists because of their extensive educations and community involvement. Memories of them will always bring a smile to my heart.

ACTION POINTS:

- John and Eliza did most everything correctly in managing their money. They didn't let relatives borrow from them, they didn't live beyond their means and they maintained a comfortable retirement.

- Their church was very important to them. They tithed regularly as well as giving generous extra gifts to the church and other area charities.

- I am so thankful he called me when he received the IRS letter rather than sending them a check and asking questions later. It would have more difficult for me to retrieve the money after he sent them a check than it was to correct the IRS's error immediately.

· ·

When a client died, I was always prepared to talk to the family about their loved one's portfolio. I would explain the investments held and what the heirs would have to do to receive their money. Some were very understanding of the process required by my firm, such as receipt of a death certificate, opening a new account to receive and transfer the assets, and many other requirements. Others would call immediately wanting to know how much money there was and how soon they could get it. People can be at their worst when pursuing money and I dealt with numerous heirs. This client's family was a pleasant surprise.

> *An inheritance quickly gained at the beginning will not be blessed at the end.*
> Proverbs 20:21 NIV

Harvey and Martie were the sweetest couple. Martie was short and plump, always smiling or laughing. Harvey was short too, but serious and he always had a smile for Martie. They were retired former mid-westerners who lived in a high-rise condominium building overlooking the water. They enjoyed social events with many people in their building and were involved in their church. I found them very easy to work with.

They had a portfolio of various stocks purchased over the years, some government mortgage bonds, and corporate notes. They were using the interest and dividends to supplement their social security income. Some of the stocks they held for many years and some had declined in value considerably. They had a sentimental attachment to the stocks but weren't happy with the smaller dividends they had been receiving.

They had two grown sons, the older one a doctor who was married with small children and the younger was unmarried, employed but not making much money. Both boys lived in another city. It was clear they were proud of their son, the doctor, while trying to give the younger son extra financial help.

From time to time, we met and made a few small changes to their portfolio, but most everything remained the way it was. Then Harvey died unexpectedly and Martie called me soon after. With his death, she had lost some of their monthly income and she was worried about having enough money to maintain a comfortable lifestyle. She had the condominium upkeep, utilities, and taxes to pay plus her automobile expenses. The dividends had declined on some of their stocks, a few of their bonds were coming due, and the newer ones had lower interest rates of return.

So, we explored an annuity that would allow her to withdraw 10% per year of the principal she invested which increased her monthly income to a comfortable level and allowed her to remain in the condo she had shared with her husband. She was happy with the results and her mind was at ease.

Martie had several health conditions that were progressively worsening so she wanted to talk to me about how to leave her assets to her sons. She felt she did not want to give an equal share of her money to her son, the doctor, because he didn't need it. She wanted to leave a larger amount to the younger son to give him a boost in supporting himself. We established the beneficiary arrangements to her liking.

When Martie died in 2005, she was scarcely buried before I received a telephone call from the youngest son asking what he should do to claim her money. I gave him the details and told him I'd send the paperwork to him. I thought to myself, it sure didn't take him long to ask about how to get the money.

Then he surprised me by quickly letting me know he was aware of how the annuity beneficiary was arranged, with him receiving most of the proceeds rather than splitting it evenly with his brother. But, he was calling to find out how to split it evenly with his brother. I reminded him that his mother's wishes were to leave it as she had stated, with him getting the majority. He told me he knew that, but **HE** wanted his older brother to have half of the estate. I was amazed and delighted that he was so willing to share the estate equally with his brother. If only other families were so principled.

I explained we would have to fill out the paperwork for him to receive the annuity and account proceeds as they were stated in the beneficiary agreement–with him receiving the majority according to his mother's wishes. That is the way it had to be paid and it was his to do with as he chose. But he made it clear; he was going to split everything evenly once he received the proceeds. It was out of my hands at that point, but I could imagine his mother and father smiling at the outcome.

ACTION POINTS:

- Dividing money in uneven amounts among children can cause problems if the children aren't aware of it. Martie must have told her youngest son what she did and that's why he knew about it and was so adamant about splitting it evenly. Sibling rivalry is difficult at best but especially when money is involved.

- Beyond that, Harvey and Martie were very good managers of their money. They were attentive to watch and understand their investments.

CHAPTER SEVEN

SUCCESSFUL MANAGERS

....

During my career, it seemed I attracted older clients, those of retirement age. Other brokers at my firm criticized me saying these clients would die and my career would be finished with no clients left.

I am thankful that did not happen. My clients either enjoyed a long life or left their estates to their children who continued with me as their advisor. However, not all clients had schooled their children to take the advice of their advisor.

Milford and Stella came to one of my investment seminars and asked me to come to their home to discuss their finances. First, I had a difficult time locating their home. 'Over the bridge and through the woods', down a hill and then I found it–a lovely home overlooking a valley of trees and a river below. Flowers everywhere and the most enormous pencil cactus I'd ever seen stood guard at the double front doors.

Milford threw open the door with a hearty "Welcome! Come on in!!" and as I entered the first thing I saw was a magnificent baby grand piano. "Do you play piano?" I asked. "Well I used to," he answered. Come to find out, he used to play quite a bit on weekends in local clubs and piano bars. He loved music and enjoyed performing whenever and wherever he could.

Milford had worked a regular job in the HR department for a large corporation and Stella worked for many years as an administrative assistant in another large corporation. Both were retired now, getting into their 80's but still active in their church and other civic organizations.

They had an investable amount of around $200,000 and they each had IRAs of about $25,000 each. They had been in CD's up to this point, so they were anxious to look at stocks to achieve some growth in the low-interest economy. I proposed a managed account plus some mutual funds to add variety and they agreed. They didn't need any monthly income but wanted to have their money secure in case they had needs later and also to leave an estate to their three children.

We kept in touch by telephone for most questions, but after a few years when I again visited them in their home, I noticed that Stella seemed somewhat confused and Milford was being more attentive to her–trying to make up for her answers when she couldn't quite respond. I felt she was beginning to fail and I was correct because in a few months Milford called to tell me they had moved into a local assisted living apartment.

I visited them in their new apartment. Although new and clean, I and was saddened to see where they had to live in comparison to their lovely home overlooking the valley of trees, but I'm sure it was a relief to Milford to have people around to help care for his wife.

About a year later, Milford called to tell me they were moving to another assisted living facility in the northern part of the state to be closer to their children. He also told me Stella had cancer and was becoming quite ill. I was so sorry to hear this and was able to visit them sometime later. I didn't get to see Stella, but Milford still seemed to be the same. However, his report on Stella was not very good. Sadly, she passed away in October of that year at the age of 89. They had been married for 58 years.

Milford didn't remain in the assisted living facility–he was still spry, cognizant, and in good physical health except for some breathing problems caused by too many cigarettes in his younger days. He was also becoming weary of being the pianist at the assisted living facility and having all the women fawn over him. He had a plan.

He wanted to build an apartment for himself alongside his son's home where he could be close and yet both could have their privacy. He asked me for a few withdrawals to accomplish that task and invited me to visit when it was completed. I did, and found it to be a functional and cozy apartment that suited him well. He had a small kitchenette, a bedroom, a bathroom, and a spacious living area. He could cook his meals or join his son and his wife for meals. He could also watch their home if they were traveling and he had the assurance of someone being close by if he needed help. It was a perfect arrangement for them both.

Milford was a wonderful letter-writer–he would often type letters to me telling me how he was or asking a question about something in his account. I've kept quite a few of his letters. His last letter typed 4 months before his death spoke about Christmas, "I had a great time with grand, great and great-great-grandchildren. The latest, 3, 4, and 6 are by all comparison the loudest. But I remove my hearing aids and get as far away as I can. I, apparently, am the only one who is bothered by the little monsters." He had a wonderful sense of humor and a remarkable mind for his age.

Milford died a few months later at the age of 96.

His accounts passed upon his death to his three children–divided equally. I met with them all once the new accounts were open and the stock shares deposited in each account.

Milford's sons had stockbrokers already, but decided to let me manage their accounts since I came strongly recommended by their father. Both were married and both wanted their accounts titled jointly, but neither wife had any interest whatsoever with what the investments were or what their husbands did with it.

Additionally, Milford's daughter had utter disinterest and allowed her husband full control of any decisions and management of the account. Since it was her inheritance, I asked her if she wanted it in her name alone, but she let me know immediately that it would be a joint account. Sadly, that was the only decision she made regarding the account.

Milford died in 2007 and the stock market did well until September 29, 2008, when it dropped over 777 points because of the failure of Congress to authorize a bank bailout and it was the second-worst point drop ever in the Dow. Then just 6 days later on October 15, 2008, it dropped again. The housing bubble also caused this. The US was now in a bad recession.

Sometime after that, both of Milford's sons moved their portions of the accounts to their long-time stockbrokers. A little later, his daughter's husband sent me a long letter citing the fears he had of the world's economy, the political party's failures, and how the 'small investor would be destroyed.' The letter asked me to liquidate their account. He ended by stating, "We agree that you have done well for Milford and for us. And we thank you for that. Unfortunately, economic conditions have been bad."

There was no reason for me to try to convince them otherwise. They were new clients to me although they had the advantage of knowing me through Milford and Stella over the years. I took comfort in knowing Milford would not have closed his account–he remained with me through September 11, 2002, when the markets closed for a week and then dropped like a rock. I always told my clients not to sell when the markets tanked–but to hold on and everything would come back up and be fine. Milford listened, but his children did not.

ACTION POINTS:

- Milford and Stella were very good managers of their money. I never heard about their children trying to borrow money or needing help with their finances.

- Milford is to be commended in planning for his life without his wife by building his dwelling and paying for it himself. That gave both him and his son their independence but they were near each other.

- Since Milford was leaving his portfolio to his children, he could have met with each child and explained to them how investing in the markets worked. He could have recounted how he didn't panic if a loss occurred but remained invested. Maybe he did and maybe he did not. Children do not always listen.

> *Even to your old age and gray hairs*
> *I am he, I am he who will sustain you.*
> *I have made you and I will carry you;*
> *I will sustain you and I will rescue you.*
> Isaiah 46:4 NIV

••

Those known as 'The Greatest Generation'–were those who had lived through part of the Great Depression as well as WWII. They were seldom rich, but always paid their bills on time and managed their money well. Of course, there were exceptions, as you will see as I contrast two different couples that were both clients of mine.

Frankie and Johnny: what can I say? They were one of my favorite couples of all my clients. Seeing them and visiting with them in their home was more like visiting with family. They were so welcoming and friendly–and oh, so much fun!

Frankie was her nickname, probably after the old song about Frankie and Johnny, but her given name was Frances. She had beautiful white hair, styled every week at the hairdresser's into a French twist and there never was a hair out of place. She had a deep, throaty laugh and a big smile. She didn't wear glasses except to read, always had her make-up on, and virtually chain-smoked cigarettes. She was a marvelous cook and played ragtime piano for anyone who would listen.

Johnny was a happy guy–always laughing too. He had been a combat soldier during WWII and had a collection of medals earned for acts of bravery. He didn't share many recounts of his heroics but once in a while he would tell a story of his daring missions and I knew he was lucky to be alive.

Frankie had been a teacher during the war and once Johnny was home, they had two sons. They raised them in their modest home in an older section of town. Both boys received college educations while Frankie went back to work until retirement. They lived a very conservative life, attended church each Sunday, and were happy and content.

We met when they attended one of my neighborhood seminars. Up to then, they invested only in CD's and were not getting much interest. We later met and discussed options for investing. They decided they wanted a managed portfolio so we chose a money-manager and the degree of risk that made them comfortable. This account allowed them to own a variety of stocks and bonds based on their values and length of time they thought they wanted to invest.

At the end of their first year as clients, they called and asked what they should do about their taxes. Johnny had always done them himself with paper and pencil, but now that they had stocks and bonds to report, he could not prepare the return. I told them I would be happy to do their return.

Later, when I opened my independent firm, with their approval, I chose to manage their portfolio myself, rather than hire an outside manager. The money manager we had previously paid no heed to their tax situation. This gave me the added advantage of being able to manage the gains and losses in their portfolio and minimize their taxes as they affected their total income picture.

Frankie and Johnny became my clients in the early '90s while the markets were very profitable and their portfolio grew very well. Then came September 11, 2001, when the Twin Towers in New York were destroyed and Wall Street shut down for a week. When the markets reopened, stocks plunged and did not recover for a long time. I made it a point to telephone all my clients when Wall Street shut down and encourage them to hold tight. I told them I believed everything would be fine eventually. Of course, no one knew what was going to happen, but selling out at this point would have locked in horrific losses. Frankie and Johnny agreed to hold on because they trusted me. I am so happy they did.

After a few years, Johnny's health began to fail. He was diagnosed with dementia. It was hard to watch his decline. His physical health was good but his eyesight was failing, his hearing was getting worse and now his memory was going. But, they were still devoted to one another and his personality did not change. He was still a happy guy.

Shortly thereafter, Frankie fell and broke her hip. She was hospitalized for surgery to repair the damage. Because she was not able to care for him, Johnny was placed in dementia care at the same hospital complex. I went to visit him once and he was so confused–he kept calling me Frankie, not realizing that I was not her. It was so sad.

When Frankie recovered enough to go home, her family hired a nurse to come in daily and care for her until she got better. The nurse also took her back and forth to see Johnny. The complex that Johnny was in had an attached high-rise building of senior apartments, so Frankie decided that she would rather live there than at home. She would have other people around, save the money that the nurse cost and be able to cross a skyway to see Johnny whenever she desired. That was a perfect solution for them all.

At this time, the sons would meet with Frankie and me so they knew what was going on with the investments. Someone would cook dinner in the apartment and we would all sit around and laugh while having a good time.

Johnny died at age 91 in 2006. I thought Frankie would be completely lost without him, but he had already been 'gone' for a few years with dementia. Once when I called her son to see how things were going, he laughed and told me that Frankie had a 'boyfriend' and was doing well. The sons thought her having a special friend was fine–since both of them were in their early 90's and both needed companionship.

Then, in about a year, her son called to give me an address change for Frankie. She had moved across town and was now living in the complex where her boyfriend lived. It was another type of elderly facility and Frankie was having a great time cooking for him. She had even given up smoking–for her health! She didn't have any health problems from her smoking that I ever heard of, but she quit anyway.

She died in 2012 of congestive heart failure. Happy to the end! I am quite sure she is playing ragtime piano somewhere in heaven while Johnny looks on smiling.

When I became their financial advisor, they had approximately $200,000 that they invested with me. When Frankie died, they had over $400,000 even after all the expenses of Johnny's nursing care and Frankie's nurse plus her time in the high-rise care apartment and last elderly facility where she moved. Both sons inherited equally and they were very pleased with my results.

But…

In contrast to Frankie and Johnny was a couple they knew that had also come to the same seminar, Daniel and Sallie. Dan was also a WWII veteran and his wife was a retired schoolteacher. After the war, they had two daughters.

Dan did not schedule an appointment after the seminar, but waited almost fifteen years to call me. When I met with them, the décor of their home intrigued me. Pieces of beautiful art covered the walls–there were souvenirs from all over the world. I inquired about their travels and they told me of all the lovely trips they had taken during their marriage. However, at this point, Dan and Sallie were not very healthy and were no longer able to travel.

Their home was lovely, in what had once been a prestigious area of town and still considered up-scale. They belonged to the Country Club and spent most of their lives entertaining and associating with affluent people.

The only problem was, when I looked at their assets–they did not have anything left. He had his military retirement and she had a teacher's retirement, but they had barely $50,000 in savings.

Dan wanted me to invest his money, hoping to make a big gain in a short time. Frankie and Johnny had bragged on my expertise and he thought I could do the same for him. However, he did not have the amount of money to be invested into stocks and bonds that Frankie and Johnny had–plus he didn't have the same length of time that Frankie and Johnny had from the early '90s. About all I could do for Dan and Sallie was to invest in mutual funds and hope the markets gave them a good return.

Nothing I did was good enough–or fast enough–so Dan removed his money from me on good terms. He was having serious health problems by now and died of heart failure shortly thereafter. I spoke to his wife sometime later and her health had broken as well. One of her daughters was living with her as her caregiver, since there was no money for anything else.

They didn't plan to fail–they just failed to plan…

ACTION PLAN:

- The contrast between Frankie and Johnny and the other couple, Dan and Sallie is evident. One couple lived within their income while the other couple did not. One planned for their future while the other did not.

- Both couples began their lives after WWII on the same footing. Both had equal post-war incomes, but both ended up with a huge difference in assets. One family was a careful money-manager while the other spent nearly all of their income and did not save for their retirement.

MY PARENTS

I cannot finish this book without mentioning where I received my financial training. It was not from a prestigious university, but from my parents.

Both of my parents were born of tenant farmers who had just enough money to get by as long as their crops were decent and the garden produced enough to put away for the winter. With milk, cream, and butter from the milk cow and abundant fresh meat from their farm animals, they lived simply but had all they needed.

They married in 1936 in the middle of the Great Depression and lived first in a small house with no electricity or running water on my paternal grandparent's tenant farm where my Daddy earned $1 per day. Later he found other jobs such as working on a new water plant installation, stringing fence wire, or shoveling the hard roads during big snowstorms. He seldom received more than $1 a day–I have a little diary with his entries to prove it. He never missed a day's work because he had a good work ethic.

When WWII broke out, Daddy was able to get a job in a small town in central Illinois, which then led to his employment by the local telephone company. Mom said when he got his first paycheck; he just sat down and looked at it. He could not believe he had so much money.

They waited until they were established with steady income to have their first child–me. From my youngest days, I remember them having very little money and living very frugally. I remember them going to the bank on Friday to cash Daddy's paycheck and depositing some money in the savings account before going to buy groceries. I had my piggy bank and was taught to save 10% and tithe 10% to church each week from my allowance. Later I funded a small Christmas Club account which enabled me to buy Christmas presents for my parents and grandparents. Later still, I had my own passbook savings account.

As years passed, Daddy was able to build a house for us–their first owned residence. It was very small, but adequate for our family of three and my parents were so proud of it. My Mother's goal was to have their house mortgage paid off by the time daddy retired. She went to business school to get training for office work and helped accomplish that goal. When Daddy retired at 65, they had no debt.

During his retirement, they enjoyed road trips within the US and spent several winters in Florida where they rented a small apartment for the 5–6 months they were there. They later sold the house Daddy built and bought another, but again, it was modest and they had no mortgage. That is where they lived until they died.

Daddy died first in 1999 at the age of 91 after a brief illness with no hospitalization bills to pay and Mom was able to live comfortably until her death almost 10 years later. Years earlier when she began receiving her own Social Security, she saved almost all of it. She later allowed me to invest some of it into mutual funds–but she just was not sure I was capable of managing her little account. I would show her the gains, but she was used to reading bank statements, not mutual fund statements, so she couldn't quite comprehend the growth. She preferred bank CD's.

After Daddy's death, she received around $700 per month in Social Security plus a small pension from Daddy's employment and she was determined to live on that amount. I set her up with state programs to freeze her real estate taxes and minimize the cost of any medication she took. She did not have to pay Federal Income Tax but still had to pay a small amount of State Income Taxes. She knew the price of every grocery item she bought, and if something went up 10¢, she would not buy it–it was too expensive she thought!

Her final and only illness lasted about 6 months during which time she was in the hospital several times, a nursing home, an assisted living facility, and finally the nursing home again. Because of the timing of her hospital/nursing home stays, she did not have to cover any of the costs except for the last partial week when she was on hospice care. She did have to pay 2 months of assisted living care even though she was not there a full 2 months. She died in March 2008 at the age of 95.

Both had pre-paid funerals and burial costs. The house was debt-free, the savings account had grown to around $100k, and it was untouched. She left instructions to gift 10% of her savings assets to specific charities, which I did as her executor. Following her final instructions and closing the estate was simple, because she and Daddy before her had made all the arrangements. I did not have to wonder what they would like me to do.

My parents were not rich in money, but they were rich in the conviction of living debt-free and planning for the future. They made sure their wills were up-to-date, their taxes paid and they never carried any debt except their home mortgage which was paid off by the time Daddy retired. They instilled these values in me and those are the riches I inherited. That's something money could never replace.

Author Bio

Carol Taylor formerly wrote newspaper columns relating to financial matters, both Christian-based and secular. She has always had a love for the written word. Carol is married to William Taylor and is the mother of two children, grandmother of five and great-grandmother of 7 and counting. She enjoys traveling, mission trips, and genealogy. Going forward she will be writing narrative accounts of her ancestors.

Carol is a strong Christian believer and gives God the glory for her business successes and His guidance in dealing with her clients as well as writing this book.

Made in the USA
Coppell, TX
31 July 2023